Podcasting
For Brands

Kurt Woischytzky

CONTENT

INTRODUCTION

Podcasts are truly a phenomenon; I can't think of another medium that has surged in popularity as rapidly in recent years. While video content has been steadily growing for quite some time, the explosion of interest in audio content has been particularly noteworthy. Ever since my early teens, I've been immersed in audio production and swiftly developed a deep love for podcasts. In this book, I aim to convey this passion to you.

The Trend Medium Podcast

Podcasts have become incredibly popular in recent years. Many people attribute this trend to several key factors. In discussions with podcasters and listeners,

four main reasons stand out as the driving forces behind the widespread appeal of this medium:

Creating podcasts is a breeze. All you need is your
voice to broadcast your message to the world
through this medium. Compared to video production,
which demands meticulous attention to lighting, settings, and various other elements, podcasting is a
much simpler process. Not only is the preparation
time significantly reduced, but post-production tasks
are also far quicker with audio-only content than with
video content.

Podcasts grab plenty of attention. This doesn't just
apply to the overall podcast market, but also to each
podcast episode. In an era where most consumers' attention spans are shrinking, podcasts truly stand out.
They draw people in, encouraging them to delve
deeply into a topic. As per a recent Bitkom study, the
average podcast episode is listened to for around 26
minutes - a far cry from the fleeting glances given to
posts on Facebook, Instagram, or even TikTok..

Podcasts are so easy to get to. You don't even need

to make an account to listen in, and there's no logging in on many apps. Nowadays, podcast apps come already installed on pretty much every smartphone, so almost anyone can tune in effortlessly.

Podcasts offer a particularly intimate experience. Many people enjoy listening to podcasts when they are free from distractions, such as during a train ride or in the quiet moments before they drift off to sleep - a profoundly personal time. After all, how many mediums can say they accompany their audience to bed? Moreover, podcasts typically reach our listeners directly in their ears. In contrast, radio or television is often merely background noise, coming from a distant speaker across the room.

In my opinion, these 4 arguments are the decisive reasons why podcasts have shot through the roof. They have filled a gap in the media industry and taken it over at record speed.

About My Background

Of course, this podcast trend has not passed me by. When I founded my company kurt creative in 2019, I was working as a full-time producer at a major German radio station and was therefore always up to date with the latest developments in the media industry. I always jokingly say that podcasts came to *me* at some point. This is because my experience in audio production meant that I was approached more and more frequently by friends from my network asking if I could produce their podcast. These initially sporadic commissions eventually grew into my company kurt creative, which has been my main source of income since 2021 and is constantly growing.

A few more facts about my career: I was born in 1995 in Dresden, Germany, straddling the line between generations Y and Z. My first exposure to media occurred when I was just 16, through an internship at the news agency dapd and freelance work at the local newspaper TLZ. I also engaged in voluntary activities at various Central German local radio stations. Subsequently, I undertook internships and freelance positions at the commercial radio station Radio Brocken. I earned a B.Sc. in Communication Management and served as a working student before becoming a full-time producer at the media production company IR Media (BB Radio, Radio Teddy). Finally, in 2021, I transitioned to full-time self-employment, establishing kurt creative as my own enterprise.

My personal content creation has been instrumental

in shaping my company from its inception. As the largest German-language YouTube channel dedicated to podcast production, it garners over 10,000 monthly views, serving as a primary resource for aspiring podcasters seeking insights and expertise in the field.

My team and I have already worked with over 200 clients to implement their podcast projects - from startups to public authorities.

The Company kurt creative

At kurt creative, my mission is to inspire customers to bring their ideas to life through podcasts and to empower them to enhance their expertise on this journey. I provide flexible services for complex technical tasks like production and publication. Rather than adhering to traditional media and agency industry patterns, my approach involves pioneering new avenues. kurt creative has evolved from a sole proprietorship where I handled marketing and production to an agency with a physical office and employees, and now to an agile, fully digital company with a strong value system, collaborating with freelancers for specialized tasks.

Our current focus at kurt creative perfectly aligns with the modern business landscape, offering flexibility, expert support, and transparent pricing. All our services can be easily accessed through an intuitive online store, adapting seamlessly to your podcasting needs.

Our Coaching and Consulting segment typically lays a solid foundation, featuring online workshops, personalized consultations, and comprehensive resources like our book. These resources prepare you for the realm of podcasting, offering essential knowledge. You can then proceed to execute your podcast project with our guidance or selectively engage our services for tasks like production, optimizing your workflow and saving valuable time.

Our services are intentionally crafted to seamlessly complement one another, providing support throughout your podcasting journey. You have the flexibility to handle tasks independently, allowing for a learning experience as well. This book offers detailed, step-by-step guidance on self-implementing your podcast, with mentions of our professional services where needed. Recognizing the challenges of explaining certain content textually, particularly software aspects, this book is enhanced by an accompanying website hosting video tutorials, downloads, and additional resources.

Aims and Structure of This Book

I skipped lengthy historical explanations about podcasts in this book since it's focused on practical application, aiming to equip you with actionable knowledge quickly.

The book is divided into five chapters:

1. Podcast Strategy

This chapter provides a foundational insight into what defines a thriving podcast. With the vast array of podcasts spanning various topics, how can yours carve a niche? What do your listeners anticipate?

What constitutes the perfect format, title, and catch-phrase? Moreover, how can you turn your podcast into a revenue stream? Addressing these queries is paramount in shaping the initial phases of your podcasting endeavor.

2. Editorial Work

After finalizing your podcast concept, it's about bringing it to life. Dive into researching timely and engaging topics, reaching out to potential guests, and setting up interviews. Get ready for insightful brainstorming sessions and learn how to strategically approach securing fascinating interviewees. Remember, not everyone who enjoys conversing is the perfect podcast guest candidate. Additionally, to ensure your initial interviews resonate, glean practical tips on hosting with grace and fluidity.

3. Recording

After prepping your content, it's time to dive into the technical side of things. While this can feel daunting initially, it doesn't have to be. I'll walk you through various setups that my clients have found effective for different recording scenarios. I'll guide you step-by-step on how to get everything ready, set up, and produce a top-notch recording.

4. Post-production

After you've wrapped up recording, the next step is all about the technical finesse: production. Here, we'll delve into the acoustic components that shape a podcast episode, offering insights on self-editing and achieving that polished, pro sound using basic technical aids. Additionally, we'll explore a sought-after area for newcomers—intros and outros.

5. Distribution

Once your podcast episode is all set to go, you're at the point where you can unleash it into the world. For many beginners, this step can seem like a mysterious realm because it's not just a matter of uploading directly to apps; you need a hosting service. This chapter lays out the straightforward steps to get this all sorted. We'll also delve into strategies that can significantly boost your podcast's visibility and help you create your own devoted audience.

Sounds exciting? I'm confident you'll find the entire process quite enjoyable. The beauty of podcasting is how it immerses you in a multitude of subjects all at once - from journalism to audio tech, social media, and marketing... the knowledge you gain here extends far beyond just your podcast. Ready to dive in?

CHAPTER 1: PODCAST STRATEGY

How Business Podcasts Work

The first crucial consideration when embarking on any project should always be: What exactly do I aim to accomplish with it? Specifically in the realm of podcasts, a pivotal query is whether your podcast will serve as a personal passion project or function as a strategic marketing asset for a business. This decision significantly shapes the podcast's overarching concept.

Personal podcasts are typically funded either by the creators themselves or through community donations, and major financial gains are not typically anticipated given their limited reach. Alternatively, podcasts by renowned individuals, like influencers, rely on advertising revenue and sponsorship agreements for income. These podcasts attain substantial viewership due to the high profile of the hosts, which attracts advertisers once a certain threshold is met – albeit this threshold is notably demanding.

Conversely, business podcasts operate as strategic marketing instruments closely tied to the company's brand. The primary objectives of such podcasts are to connect with potential customers, showcase expertise, and subtly promote the company. Even with a modest viewership, business podcasts can yield a favorable return on investment, particularly as listeners often exhibit a strong inclination towards purchasing within specialized niche markets.

Suitable Topics

Let's start by exploring the popular topics in the German podcast scene, as indicated by recent studies. Interestingly, these topics have remained remarkably consistent over the years, offering podcasters a sense of stability in planning. Making drastic changes to an established podcast's theme is usually less effective once your audience has grown accustomed to your content. However, making smaller adjustments within your niche, particularly by adapting to emerging long-term trends, is often well-received and may even maintain or increase your audience engagement.

For a significant period, the most successful themes in the podcast landscape have revolved around news and current events, comedy/entertainment featuring notable figures, love and relationships, psychology in daily life, and captivating crime stories or true crime narratives.

The popular main topics mentioned above provide a solid starting point for identifying areas where your podcast can attract a sizable audience. So, where does our podcast fit in? To distinguish your content from others, it's crucial to carve out a unique niche within these main categories. This could involve sharing intriguing crime tales specific to the Palatinate region, offering psychological insights tailored for competitive athletes, delving into the love stories of multicultural couples, or narrating amusing anecdotes from the life of a flight attendant. As demonstrated, there are ample opportunities to discover a distinctive niche within these broad subject domains. Let your imagination run wild!

As for business podcasts, how can we pinpoint a fitting topic to promote our company effectively through podcasting? To achieve this, we should initially concentrate on our company's particular expertise and the specialized field we represent. Next, we can align this expertise with one of the prominent main topics, seamlessly weaving our content into a format that not only appeals to a broader audience but also enables us to showcase our company in a compelling manner. Further insights on this approach will be discussed in the upcoming "Topic, Title, Format" section.

Success Factors

If you're dedicated to producing a successful podcast, your influence is key. Let's kick off by highlighting crucial success factors based on my experience.

First and foremost, offer your target audience **content that speaks to them uniquely**. Dive into your audience's world in the upcoming section, understanding their specific needs. Your podcast's themes should resonate exclusively with your listeners, carving out a space that's distinctly yours.

Consistency is key for your podcast's growth. Regular episodes maintain your presence in listeners' minds. Aim for a release schedule every one to three weeks. Too infrequent, and your audience might lose track; too frequent, and they might struggle to keep up. Ensure your format is consistent, setting expectations for your audience.

Foster a **strong connection with your listeners**. Dive deeper into community building in the distribution segment. When your audience feels like an integral part of your podcast community, the bond with you as the host deepens, ensuring lasting loyalty. Keep your listeners central in your content planning and creation.

Avoid turning your podcast into a blatant marketing tool, especially for business podcasts. Companies often make the error of using podcasts solely for promotion. Listeners tune in for education and entertainment, not constant ads. Integrate advertising thoughtfully within your content.

For business podcasts, **seamless integration with your brand** is vital. Establish your podcast as an extension of your brand, making its association with your company crystal clear. As a solopreneur, this can be achieved through prominent branding elements, like featuring your face or company logo, and tastefully weaving in references to your work during episodes.

The Big Balance: Listener Value vs. Marketing

The realm of promotional content is a delicate dance, and what continues to catch my eye is the tendency of companies to veer toward extremes when it comes to business podcasts. This issue warrants a dedicated discussion in its own right. As previously highlighted, the quandary with business podcasts lies in striking a harmonious balance between user value—editorial topics that pique the interest of our audience—and marketing objectives. The art of this delicate balance lies in weaving both realms seamlessly throughout our podcast.

Consider commencing with an editorial prelude, setting the stage by introducing the topic sans any overt marketing pitches. Instead, offer a tantalizing glimpse into what awaits in our podcast.

Then, gently introduce our brand within the introduction. For instance, in a recurring segment, we could subtly slip in a sponsorship nod, subtly weaving our company's name into the narrative for the first time—a soft touch of our promotional message.

Transition into the heart of our content—the interview—a moment where user value reigns supreme. Here, the overarching aim is to provide listeners with rich, pertinent content that resonates with them.

Midway through the podcast, strategically interject a product seamlessly relevant to the ongoing discussion. This tactful interruption subtly guides attention to our marketing message while ensuring minimal disruption to the flow of the interview.

Keep this marketing message succinct and to the point, saving substantial details for the podcast description. Swiftly segue back to the core content topics to retain listener engagement. Engage your audience further by hinting at what's to come in the subsequent segment to maintain their interest.

Towards the podcast's conclusion, present a call-to-action—a final nudge encouraging listeners to explore our offerings or visit our website.

Conclude with a final editorial note, perhaps teasing topics for the forthcoming episode, stoking curiosity, and enticing listeners to return next time.

By masterfully interweaving editorial content with marketing messages, ensuring a seamless fusion, you guarantee that your podcast provides value to listeners while effectively delivering your marketing messages.

Turning Listeners Into Customers

When it comes to business podcasts, it's essential to understand how listeners transition into paying customers. A crucial aspect is grasping how podcasts fit into your marketing strategy. This isn't a straightforward process; the journey to making a purchase or signing a contract can be quite indirect.

In my experience, one common question that arises early on is, "How does this investment impact our sales?" While this query is valid, it's often asked prematurely. Unlike a clickable ad on Google that yields immediate results, podcast listeners typically don't leap straight from an episode to making a purchase.

Listening to a podcast episode usually marks one of the first interactions a potential customer has with your brand. They might listen to your podcast, discover your company through an ad link, visit an Instagram post, subscribe, and only after some time, make a purchase spurred by compelling content or a special offer.

For instance, a listener might navigate to your LinkedIn page from a podcast episode, encounter your company's link, and proceed to the online store for a purchase. These convoluted journeys can stretch over weeks or months, making it crucial to allow ample time for this process to unfold.

A period of initial groundwork is indispensable. Following this, targeted surveys of new customers can unveil the various paths they took to discover your brand. Some listeners may not be ready to buy immediately but will establish a mental association between your company and the podcast topic. When their need aligns with your offerings down the line, your brand will likely be their first choice, thanks to the lasting impression created by your podcast.

Target Group

Who is the Target Group?

You likely have a basic concept of who your podcast is intended for: whether it's your current customers, potential leads, or individuals who share a similar interest. But, have you thoroughly considered if that truly encompasses everyone? I urge you to dig a bit deeper into defining your target audience. By employing strategic marketing tactics (we'll delve into this later), a podcast has the potential to capture the attention of a broader array of interest groups than you might initially anticipate. In this segment, I aim to provide a quick overview of who could be within your podcast's potential audience as part of your target demographic.

Customers

The first thing that likely comes to mind is your own customers, particularly concerning business podcasts. This is logical because customers contribute financially to the company and are thus vital for every marketing strategy. It's also valuable to delve deeper here: Do various segments exist within your customer base? Which of these segments frequently engage with podcasts? And how can we customize our podcast specifically for these segments?

Employees

For larger companies, your employees naturally form part of your audience, even if you're not directly targeting them. They are likely to tune into your podcast, driven by curiosity to understand the current focal points within the company. Questions like "What's our company emphasizing at the moment?" often play on their minds, shaping their thoughts on the organization's future trajectory. Additionally, team members might tune in to hear insights from colleagues in different departments, gaining valuable perspectives on industry-relevant subjects.

Business Partners

If you share your podcast effectively within your network (like on LinkedIn), it's highly probable that colleagues within your industry will tune in as well. I've personally observed this trend with my content: a substantial portion is consumed by individuals in my field. They frequently reach out, seeking my perspective on specific microphones, tools, and more. This scenario presents excellent chances to expand your network even further.

Investors

When producing a podcast for a startup, the investors play a pivotal role. They regularly peruse your social media content, including your podcast, to track the progress of their investment and the company's growth. A podcast presents valuable opportunities to delve deep into the company's current affairs, evolving processes, and innovative developments. Neglecting this audience can inadvertently craft an inaccurate depiction that might not align with your intentions. These instances underscore potential audience segments that might have eluded your initial planning. By expanding your outlook to encompass a diverse array of individuals, your podcast stands to achieve greater success.

The Target Group Avatar

One effective method for identifying and understanding your target audience is through the utilization of a tool called the target group avatar. I'm not
referring to the iconic movie by Christopher Nolan,
but rather the advertising industry's widely embraced approach. This tool helps in picturing the individuals who engage with a specific platform, such as
your podcast. What characteristics define these individuals? What are their likes and actions? These are
all aspects that come into play. Next, we delve deeper
into the key categories for closer examination.

Materials to the book

www.kurtcreative.com/materials-pfb

Demography

Demographic characteristics typically refer to the
fundamental data that commonly appear in studies
about a group of people. These typically include aspects such as...

- Age and gender

- Residential location (including not just particular regions, but also urban versus rural areas)
- Languages spoken (some cultures incorporate languages beyond the dominant national tongue)
- Education and profession
- Marital status
- Income

Preferences

What values matter most to your target audience? Are they all about hard work, structure, and getting everything just right? Or do they prioritize fun, freedom, and keeping it real? Each group has its own unique set of values that shape their lives.

Understanding what issues your target audience cares about in the world is crucial for shaping your podcast. Are they worried about soaring energy costs or the impact of climate change? How much do economic matters factor into their concerns? These priorities can vary widely depending on the group.

Consider the dreams and goals of your target audience. These ambitions are powerful motivators in their daily lives and affect the media they consume. Are they yearning to explore the world or saving up for their dream home?

What personal and professional plans are significant to them? Are they planning a long family vacation or are they focused on personal growth, aiming for that stylish apartment in their dream neighborhood? These aspirations also influence their career goals and educational ambitions.

Delve into the daily lives of your target audience. Do they thrive in a close-knit community with a bustling social scene, or do they prefer a more solitary existence, connecting mainly through social media?

The key to understanding your audience's preferences is engaging with them directly. You can take a scientific approach with a survey or trust your instincts by having an in-depth conversation with someone who embodies your target audience, gaining valuable insights into their preferences.

Media Usage

When exploring media consumption habits, it's important to understand when and where your target audience engages with different types of media. By identifying these interactions, we can then strategize on the most effective ways to connect with them. Understanding your audience's daily routines is key. Imagine mapping this out on a clock, marking the specific media platforms or content consumed during various hours throughout the day.

In the graphic example, the day typically starts with the radio being turned on. Next, there's a switch to using smartphones for checking news and social media. Then, it's off to work, where the focus shifts to computer tasks. During breaks, the target group resumes smartphone activities alongside computer work. Evening marks the usual time for tuning into TV programs.

This routine naturally varies among different target

groups. Thus, it's advisable to directly inquire with various typical representatives of your audience about their daily patterns. Understanding how they structure their day and which media platforms they engage with is crucial. These insights play a vital role in determining the most effective channels for distributing and promoting your podcast. Should your emphasis be on smartphone apps like Spotify and Apple Podcasts, or on integrating a player into your website? Your target group's media consumption habits can serve as a valuable compass for decision-making in this regard.

Appearance and Language

The primary communication channels your target group prefers are pivotal. Do they opt for calls, voice messages, or chats? Understanding this sheds light on the feedback platforms to offer.

Consider specific etiquettes. While some value formal address, others prefer informality. Acknowledging and adapting to these norms in your podcast is crucial.

Language nuances matter. Does slang or jargon play a role? Terms like "cringe" or "sus" resonate with the youth but might baffle an older audience. Aligning your podcast language with your audience fosters connection.

Depth of discussion varies across groups. Some enjoy light banter, while others crave detailed discourse. Tailor your podcast depth accordingly to resonate with your audience.

Certain topics remain off-limits for many groups. Income discussions, for example, are often skirted around in Germany but openly discussed in the USA. Understanding and respecting these taboos, whether cultural or demographic, is vital for podcast planning.

Using the Avatar

Once you've gathered enough details about your target audience's demographics, preferences, media habits, and language, you can create a specific avatar based on this information. Visualizing this avatar graphically and referring to it during your research for new podcast topics can be extremely helpful. Many radio stations use visual representations of their target demographics during editorial meetings to make their audience more concrete. You can even make a mood board that includes various items and settings that reflect characteristics of your avatar.

Remember that your avatar can evolve with time. As you receive feedback and learn more about your audience's lifestyle, you can adjust and refine your avatar accordingly.

Here's a useful tip I learned back when I started in radio: Keep a photo of your avatar in front of you while you present. This simple trick can naturally guide you into the right speaking mindset.

Topic, Title and Format

Now that we've delved into understanding our target audience and hopefully have a vivid image in mind of who our podcast is tailored to, the next step involves the nitty-gritty of crafting its actual design.

Podcast Formats

When considering podcast formats, the simplest option is the solo podcast. As the name suggests, a solo podcast is hosted by a single individual. This format requires minimal effort since you don't need to coordinate with guests and only require one microphone.

It works best when you have a lot to say and your topics or stories are engaging enough to stand on their own. Yet, solo podcasts can sometimes become a bit monotonous and uninteresting quickly.

Another popular format is co-hosting, where a second person joins you as a regular host. This setup can be seen in many celebrity podcasts where hosts gather to record and chat about daily experiences. The benefit is that both hosts are familiar with the technical aspects, establishing routines and inside jokes that add to the podcast's liveliness. With consistent recording in the same dynamic, co-hosting can become as seamless as a solo podcast, while the dialogue keeps the podcast engaging.

The interview format involves various guests such as colleagues, book authors, experts, and other notable personalities, covering a wide range of topics. Interviews are typically the most dynamic format and offer significant marketing opportunities, though they demand more time and effort due to varying guest needs. Some guests might not be technologically savvy, while others could be seasoned in podcasting. Nevertheless, interviews require meticulous organization but result in compelling content.

Lastly, there's a unique style known as the feature,

which is more akin to a podcast derived from radio broadcasts where pre-produced segments are repurposed. This process involves conducting interviews, splicing sound bites, and integrating scripted narrations, creating a new narrative. While artistic and elaborate, this approach is not recommended for beginners due to its complexity.

Solo-Podcast Co-hosted Interview Feature

You can easily combine different formats within a single podcast channel. For instance, you could kick off with a solo episode and transition to interviews once you become more at ease with that format. Specific topics could also be explored with a consistent co-host by your side.

Niche vs. Mainstream

When planning your podcast, one key strategic consideration is whether to focus on a niche or a broader audience. This topic is dear to me because it's often misunderstood. Some aspiring corporate podcasters opt for mainstream themes that are too broad, missing their target audience entirely. On the other hand,

I've noticed companies fixating too heavily on niche topics, sometimes only reaching a handful of listeners - needless to say, this isn't viable business-wise. A balance is essential. Let me quickly highlight the current popular mainstream topics in the podcast landscape to help draw in a broad audience.

- Politics and society (news, talk formats, history, etc.)
- Science and technology
- Health topics (especially psychology)
- Leisure, hobbies, gaming (mainly occupied by influencers)
- Nature and environment

The popular themes have stayed consistent for several years, resonating with audiences of all kinds. To leverage the widespread appeal of one of these major subjects for our particular niche, we need to pinpoint where our niche and a mainstream topic overlap. By positioning our podcast within this intersection, we can tap into a subject that captivates a wide audience, allowing us to expand our reach. Additionally, this approach provides us with the chance to establish ourselves as authorities in our niche.

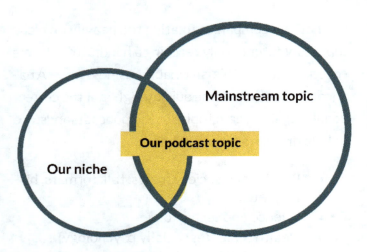

Imagine this: Suppose we aim to launch a business podcast for a company specializing in manufacturing agricultural machinery. Our focus lies in agricultural equipment, a rather niche subject attracting a limited, specific audience. To broaden our appeal, we seek to incorporate a mainstream theme. Because we have a lively host and prefer a casual tone, we opt for comedy and entertainment as the mainstream theme.

The outcome? A podcast filled with humorous tales about farm life, featuring discussions with farmers from various generations and shedding light on the quirks of rural living. This approach enables us to engage a broad audience interested in comedy podcasts while seamlessly integrating discussions about our agricultural machinery. Within this vast community of comedy enthusiasts, potential buyers of our equipment are likely to emerge. This scenario can be effortlessly adapted to different industries.

The Benefit for our Avatar

When focusing on your target audience, always consider how your podcast can enhance their daily experiences. How can your podcast add value to their lives?

One approach is by sharing insights and valuable information, such as intriguing facts or practical tips that listeners can apply directly.

Another way to brighten your audience's day is through pure entertainment. By sharing amusing stories and uplifting content, you can become a daily dose of positivity and bring a smile to your audience's faces. Shared laughter has a way of fostering connections between people.

Furthermore, your podcast can serve as a wellspring of inspiration. For instance, in the context of our farming-themed podcast, you can reach out to those who aspire to embrace rural living, nudging them to pursue their dreams and offering a glimpse into the rustic charm through your episodes.

Knowledge

Entertainment

Inspiration

Finding a Title and Slogan

Choosing a podcast name is a crucial decision that can't be taken lightly. It's a balance between crafting a memorable title that sticks in listeners' minds and aligning it with your brand or intended audience. Factors like search engine optimization and long-term recognition all come into play. While it may seem daunting, a brainstorming session can often lead to that perfect, catchy title that captures the essence of your show. Whether you're an individual podcaster or a business entity, weaving your podcast name with your brand ensures a cohesive identity. Remember, the title serves as the first impression - an artistic endeavor intertwined with strategic marketing goals.

Artistic focus

Branding focus

How can we bring these two goals together? The easiest way is to choose a creative, artistic title and combine it with our company's brand or an important keyword - if necessary, simply by adding a hyphen. This sounds trivial at first, but in practice it is often practiced in this way and has been proven to be positively received by both listeners and search engines.

Requirements for a Great Title

Apart from being creative and strategically focused on marketing, there are several other factors to weigh when deciding on your podcast title. One key consideration is its length - **ensuring brevity is essential for visibility on small screens** like smartphones, where most listeners tune in. Therefore, pivotal keywords and memorable puns should lead, not follow.

Similarly, your **title should be easy to recall** for effortless reminiscence. If a conversation sparks about podcasts among friends and the query emerges, "Hey, do you remember that awesome podcast? What was it called again?" - having a catchy, memorable title is paramount. If only a word or two is retained and they are complex or easily misspelled, the chances of finding your podcast through searches diminish. Opt for simplicity and catchiness in choosing your words. This way, most individuals will effortlessly commit your title to memory.

Additionally, **ensure your title encapsulates essential keywords** for optimal discoverability within podcast app searches. In my podcast's case, this involves the straightforward inclusion of the brand name "kurt creative" in the title, aligning with my search visibility goals. If your aim is to surface for specific terms like SEO or project management, integrating such keywords into your podcast title becomes imperative for search success.

Here speaks Kurt - the kurt creative...

"Do you know already this great podcast?"

"What was the name again?"

kurt creative

Structure of an Episode

After you've settled on the theme, title, and catch-phrase of our podcast, the next step involves organizing our podcast episodes. In the realm of podcasts, there's a tried-and-tested blueprint that has garnered acclaim, especially within the corporate podcast arena. Allow me to acquaint you with this blueprint.

Each podcast episode ought to kick off with a **teaser**. In media jargon, a teaser offers a quick glimpse into an upcoming topic, enticing listeners to stay engaged. As we're all aware, the most gripping segments often follow advertisements - a scenario familiar from radio and television. Likewise, in podcasts, we delve into an intriguing snippet from the episode before our introduction to pique listener interest. Alternatively, we may hint at the content of the episode right at the start, providing a brief, thrilling preview.

Next in line is the **intro**. It's crucial to differentiate between the intro and the introduction. The intro, a pre-produced element, resembles the catchy jingle that kicks off a radio or TV show. This concept mirrors the practices seen in popular talk shows where the intro or jingle flaunts the show's title, host's name, and possibly a slogan. Given that the intro recurs in every episode, brevity is key. Ideally, entrust a professional voice talent with its delivery to ensure it stands out. It's advisable to refrain from having the host present the intro, as this may confuse listeners and cast an unprofessional light. Hence, I always advocate for professional production of the intro or, at the very least, enlist the help of another voice artist. Feel free to craft the intro yourself or reach out to us for a range of voice actor options. Samples on our platform can guide you on the structure and tone of a polished intro, particularly suited for corporate podcasts.

Materials to the book

www.kurtcreative.com/materials-pfb

After the intro comes the **presentation** where the host introduces the topic in a friendly and engaging manner. This is an opportunity to create a personal connection with the audience and build anticipation for what's to come in the episode. If there's a guest, they are welcomed during this segment, and any necessary background information is shared.

Next up is the **main content section** where we deliver

value to our listeners. This can take the form of informative discussions, entertaining stories, interviews, or any engaging content that resonates with our target audience and enhances their daily lives.

Corporate podcasts should incorporate a clear **call to action** either in the middle or towards the end of the episode. This call to action directs listeners to a specific task like exploring further resources related to the episode, such as studies, webinars, workshops, or services mentioned. Providing this information in the show notes ensures accessibility and avoids any confusion.

To wrap up the episode professionally, we have the **outro**. This serves as the closing segment mirroring the introductory element. A well-produced outro, ideally voiced by a professional speaker, can be used to sign off gracefully and direct listeners to other platforms where they can engage further, like Instagram or LinkedIn.

Specific Elements

Structuring our podcast episodes involves

incorporating special elements in the content section. One effective addition is a recurring **teaser** that entices listeners throughout the episode, encouraging them to stay engaged. For instance, a simple prompt like "Stay tuned until the end for a special tip from our guest" can significantly boost listener retention.

Moreover, incorporating **recurring segments** adds a sense of familiarity and consistency to each episode. These segments not only provide structure but also build anticipation among listeners, especially with notable guests sharing insights in these designated sections. In longer episodes, these segments play a crucial role in maintaining clarity and coherence.

Another valuable element is the inclusion of **interaction points**, where listeners are prompted to engage directly with the presenter. For instance, inviting listeners to share their opinions via email or social media can foster a sense of community and participation. Creativity in designing interaction points can enhance listener engagement and cultivate a strong community, a key aspect discussed further in the "Distribution" chapter.

Podcasting For Brands

Teaser

Segments

Points of interaction

CHAPTER 2: EDITORIAL WORK

Research

Now that we've figured out our podcast format and
how to structure our episodes, it's time to delve into
researching topics for each show. This section focuses on the day-to-day tasks involved in content creation. You'll discover techniques for sourcing engaging guests, tips for managing your time effectively,
and guidance on being a genuine podcast host.

Brainstorming and Inspiration

Before delving into research, consider having a casual
brainstorming session. The setting where this occurs

significantly influences the flow of your creativity. So, start by pondering: Where do your best ideas typically strike? Which spaces naturally ignite your inspiration for fresh projects? Or perhaps spark thoughts about a new travel spot? Personal or professional ideas, it doesn't matter. The key is recognizing the specific places where your creativity naturally thrives.

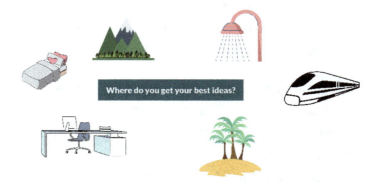

Where do you get your best ideas?

Naturally, not everyone finds their best ideas at their desks—those folks are quite rare. For most, inspiration strikes in the nooks and crannies of everyday life: during showers, hikes, vacations, or lazy days at the beach. Personally, I thrive creatively when exploring the sights and sounds of Spain, where the seeds of my future projects often bloom. The setting matters less than the ease with which you can capture these moments of brilliance. Record all your sparks of inspiration, big or small, for later review. Jot them down old-school style on paper, digitally in your phone's notes app, or even collaborate with colleagues on a shared Google Doc for some collective brainstorming.

Research and Sources

Now that we've brainstormed some creative ideas, let's dive into crafting specific events and unique angles for our podcast episodes. To achieve this, we should seek out as much external inspiration as we can. Where should we look?

Well, turning to major media outlets can be quite fruitful. These publications help us grasp global events and societal trends, enabling us to pinpoint those that align with our podcast's focus. For instance, considering the rising trend of remote work, I might explore its impact on the media industry in my podcast, shedding light on how this shift influences professionals in my field.

Additionally, delving into industry-specific trade publications offers a deeper dive into ongoing debates and hot topics within our respective sectors. In the media realm, the buzz currently revolves around artificial intelligence and the creator economy, providing rich material for podcast content.

Feedback from our audience, whether through emails, social media interactions, or face-to-face discussions, is invaluable. Maintaining accessible channels for audience feedback helps us stay attuned to the pressing issues that matter to our listeners.

Establishing an internal platform for topic suggestions—be it a physical suggestion box in the office or a digital space like a shared email account or a dedicated Slack channel—encourages team members to contribute ideas. Regularly reviewing and assessing these suggestions ensures we stay dynamic and responsive to emerging themes that may not surface during formal meetings but rather in the flow of daily life.

Leading media   Specialized media   Feedback   Internal collection

Getting out of the Filter Bubble

I always suggest stepping out of your own filter bubble when doing research. Our individual perspectives can easily mislead us about what truly matters to our target audience. During brainstorming, reflect on the crucial aspects shaping your avatar's reality. These will likely differ significantly from your personal life. Each of us resides in a distinct bubble, usually affirmed by our social circles. Engage frequently in discussions with individuals beyond your bubble—those with varied jobs and lifestyles—to grasp their current priorities. If these individuals fall within your target demographic, gauge their response to your podcast topics. This interaction is bound to spark numerous fresh ideas that might not have initially crossed your mind.

Get out of the
Filter bubble!

Content Recycling

Aside from exploring new topics, you can always repurpose content you've previously created for other uses.

If you've got published **YouTube videos**, you're all

set. You might have scripts on hand or can craft a quick bullet-point outline from the footage. This groundwork gives you a solid starting point to seek out a relevant expert for your podcast.

Repurposing **blog posts** is a great strategy for creating new content. Simply summarize the blog post in bullet points to guide your discussion in a solo episode. Additionally, if you enjoy sharing personal anecdotes, you can use them to enhance each point with your own experiences.

If you've conducted **text interviews**, consider inviting those individuals for a podcast interview on the same topic. You can also repurpose content by converting a podcast interview into a text interview using transcription software.

Internal company resources frequently contain a wealth of well-researched information that can serve as excellent material for a podcast episode. It's important to ensure that this content isn't confidential. For instance, at kurt creative, we have a standard internal procedure for establishing podcast hosting. Recently, I developed a YouTube video inspired by this process. Aspects such as host setup, given its intricate technical aspects, may be better suited for visual formats like videos. On the other hand, topics like

"Guest Research Schedule" might be more engaging for a podcast episode.

Many companies hold vast amounts of **undocumented knowledge**—practical insights accumulated over time and shared among team members. While these practices might not be written down, they can still inspire podcast episodes if they resonate with the intended audience. By transforming these unrecorded processes into podcast content, you not only capture them for the first time but also provide an internal boon for your company's knowledge base!

Coffee break anecdotes are rich with potential. These are the tales that circulate within teams, sparking lively conversations in break rooms or after hours—the buzz of the workplace. Rooted in real experiences, these narratives serve as captivating springboards for podcast content. Moreover, within your team, there's usually a perfect individual to engage in conversation on these topics.

Seminars also provide a treasure trove of pre-researched information. Have you ever delivered a seminar touching on themes relevant to your podcast? If so, leverage existing PowerPoint slides or scripts as a foundation for your research. However, bear in mind that a seminar typically covers a breadth of topics far exceeding a single podcast episode. It's advisable to segment the seminar content into digestible parts and then sift through to determine which segments are ideal for your podcast. With just the material in this book alone, you could potentially craft 20 to 30 distinct podcast episodes.

Finding Guests

Having guests on your podcast adds flavor and dynamism to your show! They bring in fresh perspectives, making your conversations richer and more engaging. It's not just about you anymore; it becomes a genuine dialogue. Plus, having a guest can amplify your podcast's reach through network effects. When your guest shares the episode, it reaches a wider audience.

These are three compelling reasons to not just stick to solo episodes but to gradually start incorporating interesting guests. This section of the book will guide you on finding the right guests, from who's a good fit to effective strategies for guest acquisition.

What Makes a Great Guest

Let's break down who makes a great podcast guest. Not just anyone who can chat will do—especially for business podcasts with specific goals in mind. Ensuring our guests align with our podcast's objectives is key. Certain criteria help with this, which I'll outline here.

First off, the guest should **resonate with our brand values** to prevent credibility clashes. You wouldn't host an oil lobbyist on a Greenpeace podcast without expecting some pushback—or without a deliberate intent for controversy. Scrutinize if the potential guest upholds your brand values, or else, why have them on?

Secondly, a **compelling, distinct story or viewpoint** elevates your episode. Exclusive narratives or unique perspectives set your content apart. Juncturally, ensure the guest is eager to share this narrative. Reluctance dulls listener engagement.

Moreover, **prior agreements on sensitive topics** are vital. It's disappointing for guests to evade key topics during interviews. Transparent discussions beforehand avoid such pitfalls.

Never let a guest derail your marketing objectives. Avoid competitors; inviting competition risks misuse or misrepresentation of your content. Seek allies from related industries instead for symbiotic relationships.

Lastly, a **guest with a broad network expands your outreach** organically. Their sharing spreads your podcast across untapped audiences, fostering mutual growth. Leveraging their name in episode titles for search engine visibility boosts discoverability.

Remember, the right guest elevates your podcast's impact while aligning with your branding and business objectives.

Guest name | 🔍

Guest - official website

Episode 3: Guest in Podcast

In the materials for this book, you'll find a handy checklist outlining the specific criteria for finding the right guest for your podcast.

 Materials to the book

www.kurtcreative.com/materials-pfb

Strategies for Finding Guests

Now that we've established the key criteria for a great podcast guest, the next logical step is figuring out where to find these ideal individuals most efficiently. Let me share with you some tried-and-true methods that have yielded results in real-world scenarios.

Without a doubt, the most straightforward approach is to tap into **resources within your own organization**. In larger companies, a simple round of inquiries among your coworkers can often reveal potential guests with captivating stories or those who are acknowledged internally for their remarkable tales. As a solopreneur, your pool of resources is more constrained, but chances are you have collaborated or brainstormed with colleagues who could make excellent podcast guests as well.

Utilize your network, both online and offline, to discover intriguing individuals for your initial podcast episodes. Peruse your contacts and identify those with captivating tales that could resonate with your target audience. Don't hesitate to inquire within your circle for potential guests or referrals.

Attending industry gatherings, such as Spotify's "All Ears" event in Berlin for the podcast community, can be fruitful. Engage with fellow attendees, strike up conversations, and explore if they have captivating narratives to share on your podcast. Chances are, similar events exist in your industry, offering ample opportunities to connect with potential guests.

After completing your initial interviews, the next natural step involves **seeking recommendations**. Towards the end of each interview, you can casually inquire whether your guests might recommend another individual from their network who would be interested in being featured on your podcast. This simple approach can facilitate valuable new connections.

When your podcast has grown in reach and influence, consider delving into the strategy of **"cold calling"** **potential guests**, beginning with individuals featured in current media coverage. Upon coming across someone intriguing in the media with a compelling story that aligns with your audience, take the initiative to track down their contact information online (as many public figures maintain personal websites or active social media profiles) and extend an invitation for an interview. The beauty of this approach lies in the fact that such individuals likely possess prior media exposure, making for engaging and seasoned guests.

Authors are frequently sought-after figures for interviews, especially following the release of a new book. This is because they naturally yearn to discuss their work across various platforms to engage potential readers. Renowned for their compelling storytelling, authors often weave intriguing narratives about their latest publications. However, caution is advised to prevent these interviews from becoming overwhelmingly self-promotional.

Exploring alternative podcast platforms that delve into similar themes is a strategy often overlooked. By **researching analogous formats within your specific niche** and identifying captivating guests, you can expand your reach significantly. Reaching out to these guests, referencing a prior podcast interview, is a common practice within the media landscape. Ideally, the preceding interview might have left certain avenues unexplored, allowing for enriched discussions during your podcast session.

Feel free to **reach out to other hosts** and propose a collaboration. This is a common practice among influencers, benefiting all parties by leveraging each other's audience. However, ensure that the host aligns with our brand values and supports our marketing objectives without compromising them, meeting the standard guest criteria.

Avoid using specialized guest platforms or Facebook groups for "guest exchange" as they often prioritize guests' self-promotion. Many aim to feature in numerous podcasts solely to showcase their products, resulting in less engaging content. Conduct your research diligently, and you may be surprised by how many individuals are willing to contribute exclusive stories to your podcast without any ulterior motives.

Furthermore, consider approaching potential guests from their perspective. Highlight the advantages they would gain from being interviewed by you, whether it's reaching a broader audience or receiving a valuable content piece they can utilize on their own platforms, such as their website.

The Guest Ladder

In the early stages, it can be challenging to draw in captivating guests when you have a relatively unheard-of podcast and just a handful of episodes out. This situation is typical since potential guests may struggle to grasp your podcast's overarching vision and what they're committing to based on a small sample of episodes. Therefore, initiating with individuals who already trust you from previous interactions is advisable. As your podcast gains traction, you can then pivot towards guests who may be more challenging to bring on board. I often visualize this progression using what I like to call the "guest ladder."

Climb the
guest ladder!

Starting with colleagues from your own company or people you already know well is the simplest way to introduce your podcast project to them. You're already familiar with their potential as guests, making it a leap of faith you can enjoy.

Moving forward, you can tap into your personal network, sharing your initial podcast episodes via social media or personal messages. This way, you create a reference point for potential guests, providing them a glimpse into what they can expect from an interview with you.

The next natural step involves seeking personal recommendations. If you've had the pleasure of hosting engaging guests on your podcast from your network, don't hesitate to ask them for further suggestions. As your podcast gains traction over time, they'll likely be more than happy to share recommendations with you.

Once your podcast has built a certain level of popularity, consider engaging with industry insiders at events and sparking their interest in your show. By this point, your podcast may have garnered enough visibility that they are already familiar with it. I once heard a story from a client who was even approached proactively about her podcast at an industry gathering.

Upon reaching this heightened level of recognition, you can approach acquisition with more confidence and even dare to connect with "big fish" in the industry, such as renowned authors or celebrities.

Presenting

Hosting a podcast can be a divisive endeavor: while some eagerly anticipate it and confidently take to the microphone, others find the prospect quite daunting. This fear often stems from perceiving moderation as somewhat forced and thus unfamiliar. Yet, moderation is essentially akin to a regular conversation. The key distinction lies in the fact that this exchange occurs not only between the guest and the host but also with an envisioned audience. In the following section, you'll learn how to seamlessly acclimate to this setting and handle podcast moderation with enjoyment and grace.

People Love People

The fundamental concept I'd like to highlight is how much people truly value connecting with other people. In this modern era dominated by virtual meetings and video chats, think back on the array of discussions you've encountered. There were those lively exchanges filled with energy and charm, where conversations unfolded in an exciting and possibly even entertaining manner. Conversely, there were likely also those tedious calls dominated by a never-ending monologue that failed to captivate even the speaker themselves. When you contrast these contrasting types of interactions, you'll intuitively grasp the key ingredients that differentiate a captivating dialogue from a lackluster one.

What Makes Conversations Interesting

In my professional experience, I've conducted numerous interviews with a variety of individuals - whether in the role of a host, a guest, or an attentive listener. Over time, I've formulated a set of guiding principles drawn from these experiences that I believe contribute to a successful interview.

One key aspect that resonates strongly is **authenticity coupled with emotional expression**. When a person engages not just in a recitation of dry facts, but also shares their emotions, it creates a far more compelling dialogue. Stiffness, insincerity, or a lack of emotional depth can quickly disengage an audience. Conversely, when a speaker communicates passionately, is unafraid to express amusement or even vulnerability, it captivates the listener. This element of genuineness humanizes the conversation, forging a natural connection that is both powerful and lasting.

We're naturally drawn to **individuals with clear goals** who are actively pursuing them. Someone who declares, "I aim to achieve X or Y within a year and here's how I plan to get there," exudes a captivating energy. Their focused determination is both motivating and contagious. On the flip side, individuals who merely discuss potential ideas to explore lack a vital component: storytelling. Narratives are pivotal for fostering connections, enabling us to resonate with others' experiences.

In this vein, we naturally gravitate toward **those who have already reached the destinations we aspire to**.

We all hold certain idols and figures we look up to. Encountering them in various media forms—be it on TV, in magazines, or through podcasts—can be riveting, almost entrancing. Their insights and journeys serve as guiding lights, propelling us forward on our own paths.

We are also keen on individuals **who offer a unique and specialized perspective** on a particular subject, ideally one that isn't commonplace. When it comes to podcast guests, I always emphasize the need for these distinct narratives. They are pivotal for an engaging dialogue, as listening to repetitive information in an interview that echoes what we've heard a thousand times before becomes tedious. It's unproductive to revisit the same old topics without gaining any fresh insights. Therefore, a unique theme or a distinct viewpoint always ensures an intriguing listening experience.

Moreover, it's noteworthy that we easily connect with individuals who **hold similar values to our own**. Recognizing this, understanding your target audience's values and beliefs is crucial. It's essential to present podcast topics in a manner that resonates with them, fostering a sense of identification.

These fundamental aspects are essential for fruitful

conversations—a realization that underscores how many of these principles apply not only to podcast interviews but also to everyday discussions. The guest criteria outlined earlier in this book encapsulate these elements comprehensively. By inviting guests who fulfill as many of these criteria as possible to your podcast—bolstered by a certain charisma and alignment with your target audience—you can effortlessly forge strong connections with your listeners.

The Role of the Presenter

In a podcast, your role as the presenter is crucial. You are the one steering the conversation, guiding both your listeners and guests through the episode. Your task is to make everyone feel comfortable and ensure that they stay engaged throughout.

Addressing the Listeners

To engage listeners effectively, start off by delving into a scenario from their everyday life. By tapping into familiar experiences, you help them relate to the podcast episode, fostering an instant emotional bond with the content.

When tailoring your communication approach, it's beneficial to mirror the language and mannerisms of your audience. Consider the conversational tone and style typical within your target demographic. While it's essential to be genuine, aligning with their communication norms helps bridge any gaps and fosters a sense of connection.

Intermittently, touch upon the values, aspirations, and desires of your audience. Whether it's the shared dream of a global adventure, a specific car they long for, or the idea of starting a farm in southern Bavaria, incorporating these themes into your podcast content can evoke emotions and deepen listeners' connection to your show.

Providing your audience with a clear structure is crucial. Help them navigate the podcast by signaling where they are in the discussion, previewing upcoming topics, and indicating the expected duration. In today's busy world, listeners appreciate knowing what to expect and how much time they will need to allocate. Intriguing teasers can smoothly transition them through different themes within the episode.

To sustain your audience's interest, infuse curiosity into your podcast content. Introduce occasional surprises that deviate from the expected norm, offering unique elements not found in every episode. These delightful twists pique listeners' interest and naturally inspire them to stay engaged and continue listening.

Addressing the Guest

Creating a relaxed and open atmosphere is key when hosting guests. Ease any tension by treating the interaction as a friendly and engaging conversation rather than a formal interrogation. Initiate some light small talk beforehand to help guests acclimate to the setting. Opt for a cozy environment over a stark office space to ensure comfort during the interview.

Promote engaging storytelling by prompting your guest to share personal anecdotes rather than delivering a formal presentation. Encourage narratives that captivate you personally, allowing the guest freedom to elaborate on intriguing points. This approach often leads to entertaining and humorous stories. If the conversation veers too far off track, you can always edit out irrelevant parts later.

Feel free to weave the guest's personal narrative into the podcast episode's structure. If the guest has shared an intriguing story ahead of the interview or if you've uncovered one during your research, consider tracing this tale chronologically throughout the episode. Begin by introducing a relatable event from the guest's life at the outset of the episode. Explore how a brilliant idea propelled the guest to their current status, depicting the obstacles encountered along the journey. This typical success story, complete with highs and lows, not only serves as rich material for novels and movies but also sets the stage for a captivating podcast episode.

Simplify any complex topics for your audience's benefit, especially when guests use technical jargon that may not be familiar to listeners. Encourage guests to explain intricate concepts in simpler terms, acknowledging that the audience may not be well-versed in the topic. For straightforward subjects, you can also provide brief clarifications to ensure that everyone comprehends the conversation clearly.

Getting more personal

Certainly, podcasts offer a great opportunity for a more personal touch! Given the intimate nature of podcasts, personal anecdotes tend to resonate well with audiences. However, drawing out these stories from your guests can sometimes be a challenge. To encourage a more personal dialogue and prompt guests to share beyond typical marketing narratives, here are some practical tips gleaned from experience.

Relaxed tone   Stories   Be playful

Establishing a personal conversational vibe hinges on maintaining a relaxed tone. Avoid rigidly reciting introductions and diving straight into questions; this can inadvertently create a formal, news-like interview atmosphere. Kick things off by engaging in casual small talk and employing conversational language. This approach sets a comfortable tone that will likely be mirrored by your guest, facilitating a more authentic and relaxed conversation.

Utilizing storytelling is key to eliciting emotions and

vibrant expression from your guest. Within their narrative lie numerous personal experiences, likely including challenges and triumphs. By prompting the guest to share these intimate stories, you can paint a comprehensive portrait of their personality, enriching the conversation with depth and authenticity.

Injecting playfulness into your conversation with the guest can be engaging. Introduce light challenges like question games such as "Either/Or?" with slightly provocative queries. You can also prompt the guest to finish a provided sentence. These playful elements stimulate creativity and encourage the guest to reveal more facets of their personality, adding a dynamic and interactive layer to the conversation.

Taking Notes

Effective preparation is key to a successful interview. The specifics of this preparation process will vary based on your unique style and preferences as a moderator. It's essential to understand yourself as a moderator. Do you thrive on thorough preparation and structured outlines, or do you excel in spontaneous, free-flowing conversations unbound by rigid frameworks? Reflecting on your moderator type is crucial, as it heavily influences how you should approach preparing for your interviews.

What type of presenter
are you?

Episode Guide

Consider creating a guide for your podcast episodes by jotting down key topics or keywords you want to cover. Avoid scripting sentences verbatim, as this can stifle your delivery and diminish spontaneity. Using brief notes or bullet points as prompts is often enough to keep you on track during recording. This method is especially useful for solo episodes and co-hosted episodes where both hosts are familiar with the episode's flow. A guide provides a sense of security and direction, ensuring a smoother and more engaging podcast recording experience.

Mind map

For those with a creative flair, consider utilizing a mind map for podcast planning. Similar to brainstorming, start by placing a central term in the middle and branching out to various sub-topics. These sub-topics can further branch out into more detailed points. During the conversation, navigate through these points, "checking off" topics as they're covered. This method allows for a looser structure, enabling you to adapt spontaneously to evolving topics while ensuring all planned points are addressed before concluding the episode.

Guideline

Mindmap

Using the Microphone

Beyond traditional conversational skills, it's crucial to consider specific technical aspects when speaking into a microphone, techniques that differ slightly from addressing an audience in person.

It's essential to maintain a consistent volume while speaking into a microphone. While you can vary your tone and expression, it's crucial to gauge how well your voice aligns with your microphone's technical specifications. When enthusiastic about a topic and speaking louder, you risk overloading the microphone, especially if speaking closely or laughing loudly, which can result in unpleasant distortion in the recording. Conduct a brief test recording before your interview to check for any clipping. If detected, adjust by slightly increasing the microphone distance or lowering the input level, if possible.

An effective tip is to hydrate by drinking water before recording. Sticky foods and sugary beverages can cause your mucous membranes to stick together, leading to distracting "smacking noises" in the recording (audible as loud clicks). While you can attempt to minimize these sounds during editing, it's challenging even with professional tools. Thus, prevent these noises from the start by hydrating your mucous membranes and vocal cords with a glass of water before recording.

When recording audio content, it's vital to speak with vivid expression and strong emphasis. Unlike videos, audio solely relies on auditory cues for perception, lacking visual reinforcement. While your joyful tone can convey happiness, visual cues like facial expressions and gestures are absent in audio. To compensate for this, amplify your emotions through your voice, emphasizing key points to engage listeners and evoke a vivid mental imagery, fostering emotional connection with your audience.

A final practical suggestion: Before recording, if you find yourself tense at the microphone, take a brief walk around your workspace or nearby park to loosen up. Physical movement injects energy into your voice, naturally enhancing your delivery with more enthusiasm and dynamism. Consider even going for a jog if you're recording in the early morning to invigorate your speaking style.

CHAPTER 3: RECORDING

Basics

The Myth of the Professional Studio

When beginners envision podcast recording, they often imagine elaborate studios with numerous controls and displays. Interestingly, some podcast agencies even promote this image, perpetuating the idea of the "professional studio," despite the actual reality being quite different. In truth, podcasts can be recorded in high quality using straightforward, affordable, and discreet equipment. Surprisingly, even major radio stations utilize home recording setups for their interviews. Don't be misled by articles featuring stock photos of music studios; these images are far removed from the practical reality of podcast recording.

The Three Factors of a Successful Recording

What are the essential elements for a successful podcast recording? Three key factors are crucial, as outlined in the following overview.

The first crucial aspect is the **recording environment**. The room in which you record plays a vital role. We'll soon discuss further details about what you should take into account.

The second element to focus on is the microphone and associated **hardware**. It's essential to use a microphone specifically designed for podcasting. In the upcoming sections, I'll present various models that are well-suited for different podcasting setups.

Lastly, the third critical factor is the **software**. You require appropriate software for podcast recording and editing. Specific recommendations for these tools will be provided in the upcoming chapters.

Recording Environment

Before delving into specific setups and their technical details, let's address a universally crucial aspect that applies to all recordings and holds significant similarities across different setups: the recording environment. It's essential to focus on minimizing factors that could impact recording quality, such as room reverberation and background noise.

Reverberation

As sound emanates from your mouth in a room, it travels throughout the space, bouncing off various surfaces. This process is illustrated in the following graphic: sound reverberates, bounces off walls, and returns, generating the familiar echoing effect. Unfortunately, this effect is often noticeable when recording in typical office or conference room settings.

To prevent the reverberation effect, it's beneficial to set up your room accordingly. Recording in a small room is one effective approach since smaller spaces typically experience less reverberation. Additionally, selecting a secluded corner of the room, somewhat isolated from the rest, can further minimize reverberation issues.

To reduce room reverberation, you can enhance the effect by placing multiple foam absorbers in various corners. These black absorbers, commonly found in studios, can be purchased at affordable prices from music stores. Nowadays, they come in different colors and advanced materials like Basotect, offering superior acoustic properties compared to traditional foam options.

Fabric curtains and textiles serve as straightforward solutions to combat room reverberation. Additionally, textile items like sofas and beds effectively reduce reverberation within a room.

In the diagram below, you can observe the process. As we speak towards the foam absorber in the corner, it absorbs a significant amount of sound energy, preventing reflection. The sound then disperses towards the adjacent curtains, spreading into the room where it gradually dissipates. Ultimately, the sound fades within the room.

By employing simple methods like these, we can create a recording environment that is devoid of reverberation and echoes, ultimately enhancing the overall recording quality.

Ambient Noise

Another critical aspect to consider is the presence of disruptive background noises in your surroundings. Common examples include noises like a squeaky chair, air conditioning hum, or a dog barking. Additionally, disturbances such as church bells, passing police cars, or general street noise can all contribute to ambient noise challenges. For instance, near my residence, a church bell chimes daily at noon. Recognizing such patterns, I plan my recording sessions to avoid these disruptions. However, if unexpected noise interrupts your recording, it's advisable to pause and resume once the disturbance subsides.

Certain issues can be addressed proactively at the start of your recording, like turning off the air conditioning or using a chair that doesn't creak. These simple adjustments help minimize ambient noise, ensuring a smoother recording experience.

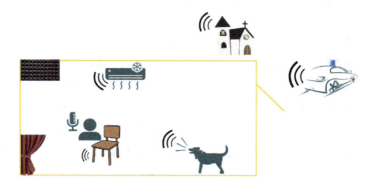

Overview of the Recording Setups

Moving on to the various technical setups for podcast recording, the selection largely hinges on the format of your podcast—be it a solo podcast, a co-hosted podcast, or an interview podcast. The technology chosen varies significantly depending on the format you opt for.

Recording solo is the most straightforward setup from a technical standpoint—simply recording in a room with only one person.

This setup can be expanded into **remote recording**. By connecting a guest via the Internet, who also has a solo recording setup like ours, we enable conversations involving two individuals. This process requires specific software, which will be further explored in the remote recording section.

Lastly, we have the setup with **guests present on-site**, where multiple individuals gather in one room for the podcast recording. As a result, several microphones are required in this room to capture the audio concurrently. While this presents an additional technical challenge, it is a relatively straightforward issue to address.

Another unique format is the **video podcast**, which presents a few technical challenges warranting a separate discussion. In a video podcast, both audio and visual content are recorded, significantly increasing complexity and altering the production process. Due to these differences, I will address this topic in a distinct chapter.

In the resources provided with this book, you'll discover a handy checklist for your recording process. I suggest reviewing it at your convenience beforehand to ensure you've considered all crucial aspects, setting the stage for a smooth premiere. Recording sessions like these can occasionally be stressful or chaotic, so it's wise to methodically work through this checklist, especially during the initial recordings.

Materials to the book

www.kurtcreative.com/materials-pfb

Solo Recording

In this section, we delve into the initial recording setup: solo recording. This approach involves recording solo, without additional guests. Solo recording stands out as the most straightforward setup, making it an ideal choice for beginners.

Advantages of Solo Recording

When contrasted with other setups, solo recording is notably straightforward and cost-effective. With just one microphone and minimal technical obstacles, initiating solo recording is a swift process. This approach

is especially well-suited for the initial podcast episodes due to its simplicity.

Certainly, conducting a solo recording while on the
move is convenient—you only need to carry your microphone and a laptop with recording software.

Using the appropriate software, you can seamlessly
transition from solo recording to remote recording.
There's no need to adjust your technical setup; simply
utilize a remote recording tool to incorporate additional guests.

Disadvantages of Solo Recording

Despite its numerous benefits, solo recording comes
with some drawbacks. In longer episodes, solo recordings can unfortunately become monotonous
quite rapidly. Without guests, it's easier for listeners
to lose interest. As a result, solo episodes should ideally not extend beyond 25 minutes to maintain audience engagement.

Moreover, maintaining a high level of eloquence is essential for speaking continuously for extended peri-
ods, as there is no external input to navigate your discourse. In solo recordings, you miss out on the back-

and-forth idea exchange common in co-hosted episodes. This absence means you must diligently structure your thoughts throughout the episode in order to ensure a seamless recording process.

Hardware

What kind of hardware is necessary for solo recording? Here, I outline a setup that numerous clients have found highly effective.

Using a USB microphone is recommended for solo recording. USB microphones have an edge over traditional analog models since they eliminate the need for an additional interface to link them to your computer. With a USB microphone, you can directly connect it to your computer using the provided USB cable, requiring no extra technology for the connection. A highly recommended option is the RØDE NT-USB Mini, a model that many of my clients find excellent for beginners, providing high-quality sound for podcasting. You can find a link to this microphone in the materials accompanying this book.

It's also a good idea to invest in a table stand. This accessory offers you greater flexibility on your desk and positions the microphone at the optimal height for speaking.

Furthermore, it's worthwhile to purchase an affordable pop filter. While the RØDE NT-USB Mini includes a basic built-in pop filter, adding an extra one in front of the microphone is beneficial. Typically, this consists of a plastic shield with a thin fabric cover stretched across it. The pop filter minimizes harsh plosive sounds like "P" and "K" sounds, which produce strong bursts of air during speech and could otherwise lead to microphone overload.

You'll also require a quiet PC for your recordings. Ensure that the PC operates quietly without producing excessive noise, such as from a loud fan, as any such noise could otherwise be audible in the recording background.

Headphones are a crucial necessity. It's highly beneficial to be able to hear yourself during recording, as this facilitates easy monitoring of the recording level. It ensures you have a clear sound, helping to avoid issues such as clipping and background noise interference in the recording.

For solo recording, including the setup outlined here, you can access a pre-made shopping list in the accompanying materials for this book.

Organization

To maximize the efficiency of your solo recordings, I'd like to offer some practical advice. For regular podcast recording, establish a dedicated recording spot with ideal acoustic properties. Identify the area in your room, office, or home office that offers the best sound quality, minimal reverberation, and reduced ambient noise. Designate this space as your primary recording location going forward. This approach ensures you're familiar with any necessary adjustments and aware of potential sources of background noise, allowing you to address and eliminate them effectively.

To prevent interruptions while recording, it's best to have your script displayed on the monitor rather than having to go through paper sheets. Personally, I prefer conducting my interviews at my desk, where I have access to my monitor. This setup allows me to navigate through the script quietly or scroll through my list of questions during the interview. If you prefer using paper, you can always utilize a script holder to secure your sheets of paper for easy reference.

It's essential to wear your headphones while recording to monitor the audio quality and catch any clipping issues early on.

I also recommend conducting a brief test before the official recording to identify and address any potential interference. By doing so, you can promptly address issues such as incorrectly connected devices or unadjusted controls that may affect the recording quality.

Software

For your solo recording software, I suggest using Audacity, a free editing tool available for Windows, Mac, and Linux. Audacity enables you to produce high-quality recordings, which can be exported as WAV files for subsequent editing and production steps, as we will explore further in the next chapter. You can access the download link for Audacity in the materials provided with this book.

 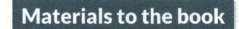

Materials to the book

www.kurtcreative.com/materials-pfb

Remote Recording

Having covered solo recording, this chapter focuses on the initial setup involving guests: remote recording. This method allows you to link up with a guest via the Internet for interviews or to record a podcast with a co-host or conversation partner.

Advantages of Remote Recording

Remote recording offers similar benefits to solo recording, with a straightforward and cost-effective technical setup.

Transporting the setup is a breeze. Simply pack your microphone and recording laptop, allowing you to record from any corner of the world with a reliable internet connection.

Remote recording allows for dynamic discussions while maintaining a clear structure. In remote interviews, individuals tend to interrupt less frequently, allowing for more orderly conversations. This behavior likely stems from the familiarity of video calls, creating a similar environment for remote interviews. Opting for remote recordings ensures a well-organized podcast with fewer interruptions.

The primary advantage of remote recording lies in its ability to facilitate discussions irrespective of location. Whether your guest is nearby, in the same city, country, or halfway across the globe, you can effortlessly connect with them as long as they have a stable internet connection. This flexibility stands as a major edge over in-person recordings.

Disadvantages of Remote Recording

Yet, remote recording does come with its downsides. A stable internet connection is crucial - at times, guests may face uncertainty, particularly when numerous individuals share the same Wi-Fi network simultaneously. This scenario can result in frequent disconnections, causing interruptions that can be quite frustrating during calls.

Moreover, the guest should possess their own microphone and possess at least fundamental technical skills to manage it. With the prevalence of video calls, most guests now own a decent headset, which serves as a suitable starting point. Nonetheless, there are guests who lack a functional microphone altogether. In such cases, you might consider providing them with a temporary device and guiding them on how to set it up on their computer. Yet, this process can prove intricate, particularly for those less adept with technology, necessitating a bit of guidance.

Lastly, the remote interview setup can be daunting for certain guests who lack experience with video calls and feel unfamiliar with them. For such individuals, the technical challenges can be overwhelming. In these instances, an in-person interview would likely be more comfortable, as the moderator takes full responsibility for handling all technical aspects.

Hardware

The equipment needed for remote recording closely mirrors that of solo recording. Opting for a USB microphone is ideal. Given that guests typically have their own computer, they can effortlessly connect a USB microphone on their end. The RØDE NT-USB Mini, previously discussed for solo recording, remains a viable option. Alternatively, another model or a reliable headset can also be used.

Once more, a table stand is perfect for keeping the microphone at the correct height and ensuring desk space remains available.

Additionally, a pop filter is highly useful for preventing overmodulation caused by plosive sounds.

It's advisable to utilize a low-noise PC for remote recording to eliminate any background noise interference.

Headphones are vital for remote recording because it's critical to hear our guest clearly. Using speakers instead could lead to the guest's sound being captured by our microphone simultaneously, resulting in an irritating echo effect. That's why it's always recommended to use headphones during remote recording.

In the materials, you'll discover a shopping list for remote recording, detailing all the technical components I suggest for the setup outlined here.

Organization

Even during remote recording, it's best to establish a dedicated recording spot. A neutral background works well, particularly for video recordings. This could be a plain wall or a roll-up/display. If you don't mind showcasing your home or office, that's perfectly fine as well - after all, it's all about personal preference.

To ensure visibility of your guest in the video, it's recommended to utilize a webcam, preferably positioned on top of your monitor. Webcam quality is insignificant in this context, as we solely focus on capturing the audio track for the podcast itself.

Both you and the guest should wear headphones during the recording session. Since most guests may not grasp the technical details, it's advisable to clarify the significance of this practice — mainly to prevent feedback and echo effects.

Once connected with the guest, conduct a brief test recording to preempt any disturbances. Should any connection issues arise during the session, it is crucial to pause the recording. Prior to commencing, you can also discuss with your guest the possibility of signaling you in case any transmission problems occur. These brief interruptions can be seamlessly edited out later, but maintaining an uninterrupted audio recording remains paramount. Therefore, promptly investigate any connectivity hitches that arise.

If the guest lacks a quality microphone, you can opt to send them a loaner device, as previously suggested. As an example, I frequently employ the RØDE NT-USB Mini, which I dispatch to my guests in a compact package for straightforward setup and use. This way,

I can ensure they have access to a high-quality microphone.

Software

Today, we're utilizing a remote recording tool. I highly recommend Riverside, a program designed specifically for podcast recording, offering excellent sound quality. It's surprising how many individuals resort to using meeting platforms such as Zoom or Teams for their remote podcast interviews, which often result in subpar audio quality. Once you've experienced recording with Riverside, you'll notice a significant difference. Riverside captures both you and your guest in high-quality WAV format, along with providing convenient additional features. Not only can you interact via video with your guest, but a local backup recording is automatically generated on your computers, ensuring a seamless recording even if internet connectivity falters. For access to Riverside, refer to the materials accompanying this book.

Materials to the book

www.kurtcreative.com/materials-pfb

Next, you can edit your remote recording using the Audacity program, which is available for free. The process is quite similar to solo recording, with the main difference being that you have two parallel tracks as source material. A link to Audacity is provided in the accompanying materials for this book. More comprehensive guidance on editing specifics will be covered in the subsequent chapter.

Recording with Guests On-site

This section focuses on the third recording setup: recording with guests on-site. Whether for a co-hosted episode or one featuring external interview guests, everyone gathers in the same room. This setup presents various technical disparities and challenges, but with adequate preparation, they are easily surmountable.

Advantages of On-site Recording

Recording with guests on-site provides the most authentic conversational setting among all setups, fostering direct interaction. This environment allows for a natural flow akin to everyday conversations, typically relaxed in nature. Additionally, it's simpler to grasp each other's remarks in discussions and build upon them. Unlike remote recordings, where discussions may involve a slight lag or require additional clarification due to transmission delays, on-site recordings are immediate and spontaneous. This spontaneity contributes significantly to the natural ambiance of the recording.

The sound quality of the recording can be reliably managed by the host or a technician, sparing guests from the task of setting up, connecting, and operating a microphone themselves.

Guests can simply relax without worrying about technical concerns, lowering the barrier to entry for many and fostering a more familiar atmosphere for them.

Disadvantages of On-site Recording

However, recording with guests on-site does come with a few drawbacks. The technical setup is notably more complex compared to solo or remote recording. Multiple microphones are required, along with tripods to properly position them in the room, which in turn involves higher investment costs.

Scheduling can be challenging, particularly when the guest and moderator reside in different towns. Additionally, travel arrangements are often necessary.

The conversation can easily become disorganized due to its high degree of spontaneity and informality. It's crucial to carefully maintain structure to ensure that both guests and, of course, listeners can follow along and prevent unnecessary elongation of the discussion.

Another consideration arising during the coronavirus pandemic involves legal or practical obstacles that hinder multiple individuals from gathering in person.

Hardware

When recording with guests on site, the hardware setup differs significantly from solo recording. While microphones are still necessary, USB microphones are not suitable for this purpose since connecting multiple USB microphones to a single computer using built-in equipment is generally unfeasible. Instead, we opt for analog microphones, typically featuring an XLR connection with three poles. I often utilize Sennheiser E 835 dynamic vocal microphones, which excel not only in vocal performance but also in podcast interviews due to their durability and ability to reduce ambient noise and room reverberations. These microphones prove particularly useful in environments with less-than-ideal acoustics, ensuring quality results and a pleasing sound output.

Each of these microphones requires a pop filter, which differs from the standard USB microphone setup. Positioned on the microphone's capsule, this foam accessory minimizes pops to a manageable level, similar to other microphone setups.

To link up these microphones, we require appropriate XLR cables. These cables are connected from the microphones on one end to an external recorder on the other.

I always suggest utilizing an external recorder for the microphones, as it offers self-sufficiency and eliminates potential interference factors like computer issues. With an external recorder, sound is directly recorded onto the device's SD card, providing multiple connections for individual microphone cables.

For on-location recordings with guests, appropriate tripods are essential. These tripods will typically be slightly larger than those used for solo or remote re-cordings due to the increased spacing between indi-viduals in the group and their varying heights that re-quire stand adjustments. It is advisable to position the microphones in close proximity to the guests to cap-ture the best sound quality from each individual.

Headphones are strongly recommended. When re-cording with guests on location, they are necessary for the presenter or a technician to monitor micro-phone levels and distances during the recording. Guests do not need to worry about this aspect; they simply need to speak naturally.

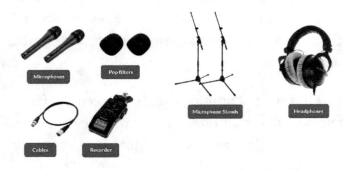

I've compiled a shopping list for on-location recording with guests, available in the materials. It includes all the technical equipment mentioned here.

Organization

For a seamless on-site recording experience with guests, thorough preparation is essential. This section outlines all the key considerations you should keep in mind.

It's advisable to locate a spacious room for all guests that also minimizes reverberations. To achieve this, opt for a room with minimal smooth surfaces, ideally furnished with items or textiles that help dampen reverberations.

Before the interview, it's important to set up the equipment well in advance, ensuring all devices are connected and tested. This setup can require 20 to 30 minutes, particularly for on-location recordings with guests which are more intricate compared to solo or remote recordings. Therefore, it's wise to allocate ample time at the outset to accommodate any potential complexities.

Upon your guests' arrival, provide a brief orientation, outlining the ideal microphone speaking distance for optimal sound quality and its significance. A range of 5 to 10 cm serves as a useful guideline for dynamic vocal microphones. Prior to the interview, adjust the recording level on the mobile recorder. You might initiate a brief test by asking your guests to introduce themselves, ensuring all technical aspects are in order.

Throughout the recording, it's important for either the presenter or a technician to wear headphones to monitor and promptly adjust the levels if a guest speaks more softly or loudly than anticipated. Additionally, it's essential to consistently monitor the speaking distance during the recording, signaling if a guest moves too far away or too close to the microphone.

After the interview, it's crucial to immediately back up the recordings by transferring them from the SD card to a computer and, if possible, creating another backup in a cloud storage service. This practice is vital to prevent any unforeseen issues resulting from accidental data loss.

Software

After transferring our raw recordings to the computer, we can further edit them using the Audacity editing program provided. A link to Audacity is available in the book materials. The following chapter will delve into practical editing methods. Alternatively, outsourcing the production of your episodes to a professional company like kurt creative is also an option.

Materials to the book

www.kurtcreative.com/materials-pfb

Podcasts with Video

Video podcast recording entails a unique setup. Given the technical disparities from audio-only recordings, I will devote a separate section to elaborate on this specific configuration.

By classic definition, podcasts are primarily considered audio-centric. However, many creators opt to record their podcasts with accompanying videos for platforms like YouTube and others. In light of this trend, it's worth revisiting the processes involved, exploring the benefits and drawbacks of this dual approach.

When incorporating video into recordings, the setup initially mirrors that of standard solo podcasting or on-site guest recording, with the addition of an extra

camera. While not delving too deeply into video production intricacies, beyond securing good audio quality, it's essential to optimize video conditions such as
lighting, setting, camera quality, and appropriate settings. Throughout the interview, the camera operates
concurrently with the audio, necessitating constant
synchronization with sound—a notable challenge
during the editing phase.

Advantages of a Podcast with Video

Leveraging a podcast accompanied by video on platforms like YouTube enhances presentation appeal
compared to showcasing only a static image or audiogram. By utilizing the visual element of these platforms, we can deliver a more engaging format that effectively captures the interest of our subscribers.

Encouraging listeners to subscribe to our various
channels is straightforward through cross-promo-
tion. For instance, we can direct Spotify listeners to
our corresponding YouTube channel and guide
YouTube viewers to access our podcast on audio platforms like Spotify and Apple Podcasts.

Using video not only engages the auditory sense but
also appeals to the visual sense, enhancing listener

retention. Subscribers can now interpret gestures, facial expressions, and the overall backdrop more clearly compared to audio-only content. For instance, a guest's facial expressions, moments of contemplation, or bursts of laughter are significantly more vivid and expressive in video format. By tapping into this additional sensory channel, our podcast becomes more dynamic and engaging.

Disadvantages of a Podcast with Video

Yet, video podcasting comes with its own set of drawbacks. The technical requirements are notably more demanding, even just for the recording stage. Managing the camera, lighting, and backdrop is a complex endeavor in itself. Consequently, the overall effort is significantly intensified compared to a standard podcast recording, where the focus is solely on audio production.

Moreover, editing audio and video in tandem is a more intricate process. Ensuring synchronization between video and audio elements adds complexity to editing. While removing specific segments in a pure audio podcast is straightforward, the presence of "image jumps" in video editing typically necessitates multiple camera angles to address. Such challenges are generally not encountered in audio editing tasks.

A quality microphone plays a crucial role in audio quality. Yet, in video recordings, certain microphone models can obstruct your face, posing a potential distraction. While this might not be an issue for audio-centric podcasts and could even enhance authenticity, it becomes problematic for video podcasts where visual engagement is key. In such cases, using a large studio microphone can detract from the viewing experience. Opting for a less obtrusive microphone, though providing inferior sound, is often necessary to ensure a visually unobstructed recording.

When preparing for a video interview, guests may shift their focus towards appearance rather than solely on the content message. The desire to present well on video could potentially detract from their content delivery. In contrast, individuals tend to be more authentic in audio podcasts as they feel less scrutinized, placing less emphasis on appearances.

As observed from the comparison, allocating 100% effort to both video and audio is a challenging feat. It's essential to prioritize one over the other. Personally, I firmly believe that striving for optimal outcomes in both realms simultaneously is not feasible.

Prioritizing audio quality means that video becomes more of a secondary consideration. While you'll achieve excellent sound, there may be some compromises in video presentation, such as a visible microphone in the frame or a more technical backdrop.

Conversely, if the emphasis is on video quality, audio sometimes takes a back seat. In such cases, you might opt for a discreet clip-on microphone that minimally interferes with the visuals but compromises sound quality. Alternatively, prioritizing seamless video flow might result in the inclusion of pauses, background noises, or filler words in the final episode.

The decision of whether to podcast with or without

video is a nuanced one that warrants thoughtful consideration. Additionally, you have the option to utilize
an audio-only podcast on YouTube by generating an
audiogram. Further details on this can be explored in
the "Distribution" chapter.

CHAPTER 4: POST-PRODUCTION

After finalizing your initial recording, the next step involves transitioning to the production phase. Within this section, I'll guide you through the various stages from the raw recording to a polished podcast episode primed for broadcast across popular platforms.

Production Process

The podcast production process consistently adheres to a specific pattern, one that I'd like to walk you through step by step.

An initial crucial step involves **backing up audio files** from your external recorder, online tool, or computer. While it might seem straightforward, mishaps like accidental deletions or file confusion are common with remote recordings. Therefore, it's essential to promptly back up and organize all files post-recording to ensure they are readily accessible for subsequent production steps.

Next, the **files might require conversion into the correct format**. Recordings from remote recording tools may not be in a readily usable format like WAV or MP3 but rather in formats like FLAC or M4A. Consequently, the initial task is to convert these files into a universally compatible format, with the preferred standard being the lossless WAV format.

Next comes the **editing phase**, where we trim our podcast episode. We meticulously review the entire episode, identifying and removing any undesirable sections like slips of the tongue, abrupt beginnings, filler words, or extended pauses to refine the recording.

With the content and style edits done, we now focus on achieving great audio quality. The process starts with **mixing**, where we balance the volume levels of our tracks by elevating quieter segments and diminishing louder portions. This ensures a seamless and balanced sound throughout the entire recording.

Following mixing, we move on to the **mastering stage**. Here, we employ tools like the equalizer, compressor, and limiter to enhance our mixed recording's sound quality, ensuring consistency and denseness. For instance, we can slightly amplify the treble for muffled voices or reduce it for overly sharp voices, tailoring the sound to be more pleasing. Mastering offers us various techniques to refine the audio for optimal quality.

Once we have completed the mastering of our podcast episode, we can proceed to export it and then **upload the finalized episode**. This involves uploading it to our podcast host and submitting it for publication on the selected podcast platforms. Detailed instructions on this process can be found in the following chapter titled "Distribution".

Once you've gained some experience, you can handle this entire process independently using the free editing program, Audacity. Alternatively, you have the option to outsource the production to a specialized company like kurt creative. We provide adaptable editing rates for podcast editing services, involving the cutting, mixing, and mastering of your raw recordings to meet the highest technical standards for publication. This approach saves you valuable time that can be allocated to other tasks. For more details about our editing services, refer to the supplementary materials associated with this book.

Intro, Outro, Audio Branding

Additional key aspects of your podcast production include the introduction, conclusion, and overall audio branding. In this segment, I'll elaborate on their significance and why these elements play a crucial role in the podcasting process.

The **intro** serves as a consistent auditory identifier that opens each podcast episode, sometimes known as a jingle. This segment provides your podcast with a recognizable touch and significantly enhances its professionalism. Typically, it comprises a speaker's recording accompanied by background instrumental music (referred to as a "music bed") and may also incorporate succinct sound effects.

Ideally, the intro should include essential details about the podcast, such as its name, slogan, and the presenter's name. It's crucial not to overwhelm it with excessive information, as this could deter regular listeners. The optimal length ranges from 10 to 15 seconds. The intro is crafted once and then reused in every subsequent podcast episode.

The **outro** serves as the counterpart to the introduction and is featured at the conclusion of every podcast episode to provide a fitting acoustic closure. The style should align with that of the introduction, allowing for elements such as a call to action or a link to your website to be seamlessly integrated.

Audio branding extends to encompass **music beds**, instrumental pieces of music that accompany voice recordings in the background. Music beds can be employed to accentuate specific recurring sections within your podcast, effectively setting them apart from the rest of the episode.

In the supplementary materials for this book, you'll discover an appropriate text template for the intro and outro that has proven effective in my practical experience. I suggest that the presenter refrains from voicing the intro and outro to maintain a neutral tone, allowing these elements to serve their purpose as distinct branding components.

Quality Factors for Intro and Outro

"First impressions matter," and this holds true for your podcast as well. Regrettably, I frequently come across podcasts with inadequately produced intros and outros, resulting in a negative impact within the initial moments of each episode. Hence, I've set aside this particular section to address the essential elements that contribute to crafting a quality introduction and conclusion.

As highlighted earlier, the intro and outro serve as neutral branding components and should not be voiced by the presenter to prevent potential confusion when the presenter self-identifies. Such an approach can befuddle listeners and is best avoided. The sole scenario where a presenter's self-introduction within the intro can be warranted is for a brief introduction in the first person, limited to the inaugural episode only.

When recording the intro, it's advisable to engage a

professional voice-over artist whose style aligns with the branding of your company. For youthful companies, a vibrant and youthful voice works well. Conversely, if your brand emphasizes trust and tradition, opting for a more mature-sounding voice can help underscore these values effectively.

Naturally, the music selection should align with your brand image and be uniform for both the intro and outro. To maintain a cohesive audio branding throughout your podcast, other music beds within the episodes should also uphold a similar style, possibly achieved through musical variations of the intro.

To ensure a seamless listening experience for regular listeners, it's essential that the intro conveys only vital information and lasts no longer than 15 seconds.

My final suggestion, encompassing all the points covered above: Opt for professional production of the intro and outro. This singularly crafted branding component will endure throughout your podcast's lifespan, making it a vital and enduring investment. At kurt creative, we collaborate with a wide array of professional voice artists and have crafted polished intros and outros for diverse podcasts. Referencing the materials accompanying this book, you'll discover a link to our overview page, presenting a range of demos for previously created intros.

Production with Audacity

You have the option to entrust the production of your podcast episode to a professional company like kurt creative or undertake the process yourself. For a DIY approach, the free editing program Audacity is well-suited for managing all tasks from crafting the intro and outro to editing, mixing, mastering, and exporting. The download link is provided in the supplementary materials accompanying this book.

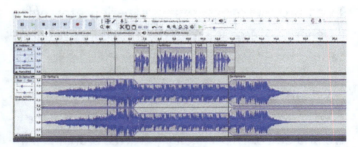

Production of an intro using Audacity

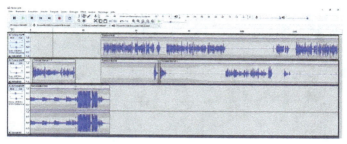

Mixing a podcast episode using multiple tracks

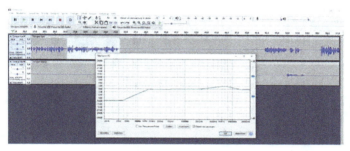

Adjusting frequency differences with the equalizer

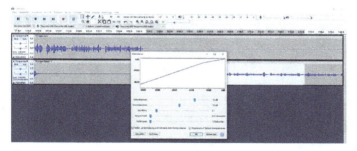

Compressing a quiet sound track with the compressor

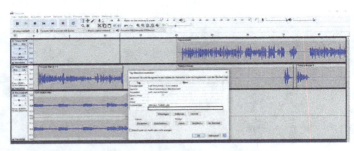

Export the finished episode as an MP3 file

Materials to the book

www.kurtcreative.com/materials-pfb

CHAPTER 5: DISTRIBUTION

Podcast Appearance

Apart from the audio content, how you present your podcast significantly influences its success. This chapter will begin by outlining the basic structure of a podcast channel. Subsequently, we will delve into specific elements: crafting the podcast description, titling episodes, creating show notes, designing visuals (graphics), and lastly, covering the podcast trailer—a unique feature offered by certain podcast platforms like Spotify and Apple Podcasts.

Structure of the Channel

A podcast channel typically comprises similar compo-
nents, irrespective of the application being utilized.
The screenshot below illustrates an example from the
Spotify app.

The initial focal point is the **podcast name**. We previously delved into the intricacies of selecting an ideal
podcast name in the content chapter, outlining the
most suitable types of names and key considerations
for making a choice.

In most applications, you'll locate the **podcast description** just below the podcast name. This brief introductory text aims to pique the interest of your audience, offering insights into the podcast's theme, typical guest profiles, and target audience.

Moving on to individual episodes, each episode is typically accompanied by a **title** and additional descriptive text known as episode **shownotes**.

With an understanding of the fundamental layout of a podcast channel and the distinctive aspects of its individual components, let's now delve deeper into each of these elements.

Podcast Description

Aim for **brevity and conciseness** in your podcast description, ideally within a maximum of 600 characters. Longer texts may get truncated on various platforms, and most listeners typically prefer shorter descriptions due to time constraints. The primary goal should be to encourage listeners to start engaging with the initial episode swiftly.

Craft your description to **spark curiosity about your podcast** from the outset. Leave some questions unanswered intentionally and refrain from providing all the details in the description. This technique, known as "teasing" in media contexts, entices listeners to tune in to your podcast rather than skipping to another format.

Include **SEO-relevant keywords** in your description, referring to specific terms you aim to be associated with in search engine results. However, ensure a balanced use of these keywords and avoid "keyword stuffing," which involves excessive repetition of certain terms. Many search engines view this as manipulative and may penalize your ranking as a result.

When publishing on platforms like **iTunes and Spotify**, choosing an appropriate category is crucial. This selection can be made from a predefined list within your Podcast Host. I delve into this process more extensively in the podcast host section. Numerous listeners explore new podcasts using category searches within podcast apps, underscoring the significance of accurately listing your podcast in the correct category.

Including links to your other channels—such as your website, YouTube channel, or social media profiles—in the podcast description is highly beneficial. Legal requirements like an imprint and data protection information may also be necessary. These links not only drive additional traffic to other platforms but also contribute to better growth and visibility across different channels for your content.

Title of the Episodes

Selecting an engaging episode title is crucial for attracting potential listeners to your podcast episodes. Below, you'll find a screenshot showcasing some examples of compelling episode titles.

A **touch of clickbait is permissible**. By intriguing your audience, their curiosity about the episode's content will be piqued. Identify statements in your podcast episode that appear remarkably surprising to your target audience or seem contradictory, and leverage them as hooks for crafting compelling episode titles.

Including the **guest's name or their company in the title** is crucial. This practice aids in search engine optimization, particularly for garnering traffic from major search engines, especially when featuring celebrities or well-known figures in your industry. Prospective listeners might conduct targeted searches for your guests, leading them to discover your podcast. Regularly hosting celebrity guests can significantly boost your viewership and engagement.

Similar to podcast descriptions, **including common search terms from your industry** in the podcast title can greatly aid search engine optimization. For instance, in a podcast focusing on audio production, integrating keywords like microphone and studio into the title can enhance the chances of ranking higher in relevant search results.

Limit titles to ten words for readability on all devices. Avoid cutoffs on small screens.

I suggest **avoiding using episode numbers in the title**. In the past, it was a popular practice to start each new episode with a sequential number. However, since Apple Podcasts already applies its own numbering in specific views and because it can create confusion when episodes are removed later on, Apple recommends against this practice. There have been in-stances where episodes with numbering have faced potential ranking downgrades.

Shownotes

The text accompanying each podcast episode is re-ferred to as the show notes. In this section, you have the freedom to include a more extensive amount of text compared to the podcast description. It's recom-mended to limit the show notes to a maximum of 4000 characters. An effective strategy is to **kick off these notes with an engaging, possibly provocative opening sentence** to captivate the interest of poten-tial listeners. In many applications, only the initial two or three lines of the show notes are visible initially (with the option to expand the full text by clicking a button), making a compelling introduction crucial in encouraging further exploration by the audience.

Avoid using HTML formatting for your show notes. While some podcast hosting platforms allow you to use bold, underline, italics, or even include images, many podcast applications might not render this HTML formatting correctly. In the worst-case sce-nario, it could lead to display errors in certain apps.

Following the introduction, it's advisable to **provide a**

concise summary of the episode's themes in the main body of the show notes. However, it's important not to reveal everything; leaving some key details undisclosed can pique the interest of potential listeners and compel them to listen to the complete episode.

Utilize **lists, paragraphs, and empty lines** to effectively structure your show notes. Ensure that your formatting enhances readability and avoids long blocks of uninterrupted text. Mixing bullet-point lists with standard paragraphs can help to organize your content and make it more engaging for the audience.

Consider optimizing your show notes for search engines by **incorporating relevant industry-specific keywords**. This practice can enhance the discoverability of your podcast episodes in search results.

I recommend **including links** at the end of your show notes, directing listeners to the guest's social media profiles or podcast. This simple addition facilitates easy access to additional information about your guest, while also driving traffic to their respective channels.

Visuals

Visuals encompass all graphics associated with the podcast, prominently featuring the podcast cover. This cover art is showcased alongside the podcast title in various areas such as the podcast description, search results, and podcast charts.

Podcast cover

The podcast cover serves as a visual representation of the entire podcast channel. In the collage provided, you can observe various examples of podcast covers from my clients. You will likely notice certain commonalities: vibrant colors, captivating graphics or faces, and a clearly visible podcast title. These elements play a crucial role as the podcast cover should instantly capture attention and make an impact at a glance.

Apart from the podcast cover, there are also individual episode images that represent specific podcast episodes. It's recommended that these images align with the overall design aesthetic of the podcast cover. Below, you can view two examples of episode images from podcasts created by my clients.

Episode image

In both instances, the guest's faces stand out prominently. For the 9 Meter 15 podcast, the guest's name is featured, while the ITONICS podcast includes the interviewer's company logo. These elements enhance personalization and connection with the guests. For instance, if someone searches for Benedikt Kempkers, they'd instantly recognize the podcast by its unique cover, spot a familiar face, and are more inclined to click on it compared to a generic cover lacking personal touches.

Tips for Great Podcast Covers

All visual elements should feature an attention-grabbing photo, with faces being particularly effective as eye-catching focal points for viewers. To reinforce brand recognition, align the color schemes and fonts with your corporate design or logo colors.

When incorporating text on the cover, opt for a concise message in a large font size. Limit the amount of text to ensure readability, especially since podcasts are commonly accessed on smaller screens where overly small fonts can hinder legibility. Clarity should always take precedence in design choices.

If you have a logo, it's essential to incorporate it into your podcast cover. A separate logo specifically for the podcast isn't necessary; the goal is to reinforce your company brand through the podcast. For individuals running their own businesses, a portrait photo is a suitable alternative.

When creating visuals, opt for the widely compatible JPEG format with dimensions of 3000 x 3000 pixels. This format is universally supported by various hosting platforms and can be seamlessly processed across different services.

Podcast Trailer

The podcast trailer, found on Spotify and Apple Podcasts apps, functions as an auditory teaser for your podcast. Similar to show notes, it features its own title and a brief description. Typically lasting between 2:00 to 2:30 minutes, the trailer offers a snapshot of your podcast's essential highlights and key information.

The trailer is prominently positioned at the top of Spotify, right beneath the podcast description. It often serves as an initial point of contact for many listeners, influencing their decision to explore further podcast episodes. The structure and content of your trailer can vary based on factors like whether your podcast is newly launched or if multiple episodes are already available online.

Launch Trailer

For a newly launched podcast, a great starting point is what I like to refer to as a "launch trailer." Given that there's no existing audio content from completed episodes, this trailer mainly features a moderator-style introduction. Structured akin to a podcast episode, you briefly discuss the podcast's theme, title, publishing frequency, and other essential details in a casual manner. Enhanced by a fitting music bed, such as your podcast intro, this approach ensures a cohesive audio branding experience.

Original Sound Trailer

After releasing 5 to 10 episodes and accumulating sufficient audio content from your interviews, you can transition to creating an original sound trailer. This type of trailer comprises snippets known as original sounds, a standard media term. These excerpts are brief segments extracted from previous podcast episodes and woven together into a collage. The original sound trailer offers listeners an authentic preview of what they can anticipate in your podcast.

For guidance on structuring both the launch trailer and the original sound trailer, refer to the templates provided in the accompanying materials for this book.

Podcast Hoster

Having delved into the content and visual design of a

podcast channel in previous sections, this segment focuses on the technical aspects. This involves leveraging a podcast hosting service. Think of the hoster as akin to a web server where all your podcast materials reside: your podcast episodes saved as MP3 files, episode images, podcast cover, titles, show notes, and more. This information is stored on the hosting service and disseminated to different podcast applications. In this chapter, you will grasp how to establish the hoster and establish connections with podcast apps.

Functionality

How exactly does a podcast reach your audience? This process might seem unfamiliar initially, especially since podcast distribution differs significantly from social media platforms. Podcasts aren't directly uploaded to platforms like Apple Podcasts or Spotify; instead, they are initially uploaded to a podcast hosting service, which then disseminates them to podcast apps through an interface.

The hosting service compiles all files into a machine-readable directory known as the RSS feed. This feed is subsequently transmitted to podcast apps and is routinely monitored by them for any new content.

Thus, it is crucial to configure the hosting service correctly to ensure that your podcast consistently appears across all platforms.

Overview of Different Hosters

Today, there is a wide array of hosting services available, each offering similar foundational features. Distinctions among them typically revolve around pricing structures, analytics capabilities, and monetization options. Hosters requiring a subscription fee include platforms like Libsyn, Buzzsprout, and Podbean.

Anchor is a commonly utilized hoster, recently acquired by Spotify and rebranded as "Spotify for Podcasters." As of the publication of this book, utilizing Anchor comes at no cost.

Alternatively, you have the option to manually generate an RSS feed on your personal server, such as through a Wordpress plugin. Nonetheless, this approach is more intricate and involves navigating technical complexities.

Statistics in the Hoster

Analytics play a crucial role across nearly all hosting platforms. They are indispensable for podcasters, providing essential insights to gauge the performance of individual episodes. Most hosting services now furnish fundamental statistics, including metrics like view counts, geographical origin of viewers, and the most commonly used apps for accessing the content.

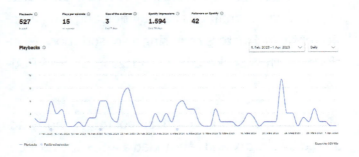

Within many hosting platforms, you can also identify which podcast episodes garnered notable popularity among listeners.

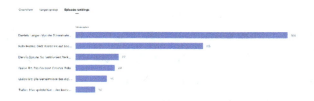

Geographical insights and data regarding the pre-ferred apps are valuable for obtaining a detailed over-view of distribution channels. This information can help in determining which podcast platforms are es-pecially effective for promoting your content.

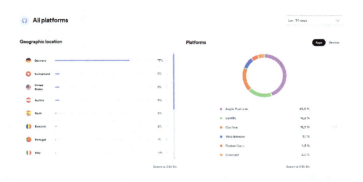

Statistics in Spotify

Apart from the overarching statistics provided by the podcast hosting service, individual podcast platforms also offer specific analytics. For instance, with Spotify, you can access these insights through the Spotify for Podcasters platform.

Within Spotify for Podcasters, you gain access to demographic information about your listeners. This data is particularly precise due to Spotify users voluntarily sharing details such as gender, age, and musical preferences when setting up their accounts. Consequently, this information enables you to draw valuable insights into the demographics of your target audience.

Statistics in Apple Podcasts Connect

Apple Podcasts offers a comparable platform known as Apple Podcasts Connect. Through this portal, you can access additional valuable insights about your podcast and individual episodes, including the listen-through rate. This metric helps you pinpoint where listeners disengaged from your podcast, indicating sections that may have been less engaging. By discerning these patterns, you can make informed assessments about the quality of your content.

Special Case: Internal Podcast

I'd like to highlight a unique category known as internal podcasts. In contrast to public podcasts utilized for marketing, internal podcasts cater to closed user groups, serving purposes like training initiatives or fostering communication within companies. Internal podcasts markedly diverge from traditional public podcasts, particularly in terms of their distribution channels. Let's delve further into this distinguishing feature.

The objective of a **public podcast** is to achieve broad distribution across multiple platforms, ensuring easy accessibility on relevant apps. This is technically accomplished by uploading files to a hosting service, which are then disseminated to various platforms through the RSS feed. Since the RSS feed is public, anyone can access the files and episodes.

Conversely, with **internal podcasts**, the focus is on reaching a specific target audience exclusively. This entails catering to a delimited user group, such as employees of a particular company or subscribers to a newsletter. To regulate access to the podcast content, measures like intranet utilization or secure apps and websites with password protection are implemented to prevent unauthorized access. Monitoring the success of internal podcasts typically involves tracking file views on the server. Unfortunately, more detailed statistics like viewers' countries of origin or demographic data commonly available in platforms like Spotify are not readily accessible. However, due to the focused nature of internal podcasts, obtaining direct feedback from the intended audience is often more straightforward.

Many companies opt for internal podcast distribution through their intranet, which inherently possesses access controls, or via dedicated password-protected login areas on their websites.

Some hosting providers offer the capability to establish a protected feed. With this setup, listeners can visit a designated page on the hosting platform, input a password, and gain access to the podcast.

Another avenue is the development of a custom app. This route is particularly fitting for larger enterprises with adequate financial resources. Such an app can be internally circulated to all company employees and customized to align closely with the organization's specific requirements.

Setting up the Hoster

The technical setup process for the hosting service can vary significantly among different providers. Detailed guidance on this procedure can be found in the accompanying materials for this book.

Similar to most online services, setting up an account with the hosting provider typically necessitates the input of standard information like email address, name, password, and other relevant details.

Next, you'll be prompted to input specific details about the podcast, including its name, description, category, cover photo, and other pertinent information.

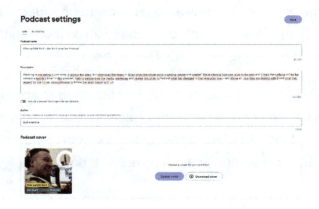

Following that, it's time to upload your inaugural epi-

sode. You'll require your edited and mastered recording saved as an MP3 file, along with the title, show
notes, and optionally, an episode image.

Once your podcast is configured and the initial episode (and potentially a trailer) is uploaded, the next
step is to connect it with various podcast platforms.
It's crucial to establish links with major platforms like
Spotify and Apple Podcasts. Other popular apps in
German-speaking regions include Amazon Music,
Google Podcasts, and Deezer. Most platforms now
offer a straightforward one-click integration option
via the hosting service.

For Apple Podcasts, however, you'll need to manually
submit the RSS feed through the Apple Podcasts Connect portal.

Several hosting platforms provide a feature known as a podcast blog, where your most recent episodes are automatically showcased. This blog can typically be customized to match your preferences, allowing you to select colors, fonts, logos, and more. It can serve as a temporary substitute for a complete website, particularly in the initial stages. Alternatively, if you have an existing website, you can utilize embed players available on the hosting platform. These players can be integrated into your website using HTML code.

Create account and basic setup

Upload of the first episode and the trailer

Linking with Spotify, Apple Podcasts, Amazon Music, Google Podcasts and Deezer

Podcast blog and embed player

The Spotify platform provides exclusive additional features that were once exclusive to the in-house Spotify hosting service, Anchor (now "Spotify for Podcasters"). These features include the ability to upload video podcasts, generate playlists combining podcast segments and music, and incorporate polls. Since these functions are not widely utilized as of the publication of this book (Spotify being predominantly recognized as a music and audio streaming platform), I will not delve further into them.

Apps and Platforms

Having familiarized yourself with the fundamental technical process, from uploading a podcast episode to its publication on podcast apps, the subsequent section will delve into an in-depth examination of specific podcast applications.

Role and Overview of the Platforms

Let's focus on the platforms that hold significant popularity. Notably, the Online Audio Monitor, an investigation conducted by the state media authorities in Germany, provides valuable insights into this landscape.

Unsurprisingly, **Spotify** dominates this market, commanding a sizable 48% share. Given this status, actively integrating with Spotify in your promotional efforts and promoting it as a viable podcast listening platform is highly recommended.

Following closely is **Amazon Music**, claiming a 21% share. This placement might surprise some, given the app's relatively lesser-known status. However, Amazon Music's statistics encompass downloads initiated through Alexa devices, which possess a podcast skill activating the Amazon Music app in the background upon command, such as "Alexa, play podcast XYZ."

Apple Podcasts holds the third position in popularity at 12%. It secures the top spot on iPhones, as it is a pre-installed app on all Apple devices, widely used by most iPhone users. Given that individuals with higher incomes often prefer iPhones, Apple Podcasts proves to be highly relevant for marketing to specific demographic segments, making it advantageous to link to this platform.

Google Podcasts, with a 9% market share, functions primarily as an aggregator of publicly available podcasts and remains relatively obscure. Although utilized by a minority of users, it comes pre-installed on numerous Android phones, offering a comparable advantage at the outset similar to Apple Podcasts.

Similarly evolving from a music streaming background, **Deezer** sits at 7%. While the platform strives to build recognition through exclusive podcasts and curated lists, its reach remains limited at the moment, making it a negligible factor in marketing strategies.

Other Distribution Channels

Beyond traditional podcast apps, there are other overlooked channels serving as potent distribution mediums for podcasts, commanding significant market shares deserving acknowledgment.

Leading the pack is **YouTube**, boasting a 44% market share. Positioned as the second most influential podcast platform broadly following Spotify, YouTube hosts a multitude of podcast content, including video podcasts and influencer interview series. Although the term "podcast" may seem somewhat blurred in this context, leveraging YouTube is highly recommended given its vast audience potential, at the very least as an auxiliary content dissemination outlet. You have the option to upload your audio content on YouTube accompanied by a still image or audiogram presented in video format.

The **company's own website** is frequently overlooked as a distribution channel for podcasts. Surprisingly, 16% of individuals opt to listen to podcasts not through apps but via dedicated websites such as those maintained by companies, publishers, or radio stations. These websites commonly incorporate embedded podcast players, presenting a valuable opportunity for podcast creators to leverage. Most podcast hosting services provide embedded players that allow you to integrate an HTML code into your website, enabling you to showcase a visually appealing podcast player designed to match your site. This setup facilitates direct podcast consumption on your website, eliminating the need for users to navigate elsewhere for listening.

Presently, there is no distinct data available concerning **smart speakers** like Amazon Alexa. Nevertheless, being present on platforms such as Amazon Music and Google Podcasts ensures visibility on Amazon Alexa devices and Google Home speakers.

Similarly, there is a lack of data pertaining to **proprietary apps**, which typically occupy a niche space. While some major corporations maintain apps that aggregate and consolidate specific content, this approach is not yet beneficial for smaller companies.

Charts and Algorithms

Don't Compare with Mainstream Podcasts

An often-raised question concerning podcast apps pertains to the charts and their compilation process. The podcast charts, while shrouded in some mystery for many, are fundamentally computed akin to trends on platforms like YouTube or the general airplay charts in radio broadcasting. The frequency of podcast listens directly influences its popularity in the algorithm, thereby elevating its ranking. However, it's important to exercise caution against applying double standards in this context. Comparisons between a prominent mainstream format featuring celebrities and a niche or corporate podcast may not be entirely

fair or accurate due to differing audiences and objectives.

Top Podcasts   **Specialized Podcasts**

To draw a fitting analogy, let's consider discotheques
and bars. In every city, you'll find mainstream clubs
playing the latest pop tunes that cater to the broadest
audience's tastes. Many individuals frequent these
venues for a lively night with friends, dancing to popular tracks. However, it's rare to hear someone ex-
claim after a club visit, "I had such a great time hearing
the latest hits from Justin Bieber and Lady Gaga." This
scenario parallels the phenomenon observed with
popular top podcasts—they attract a large audience
yet often fail to cultivate a deep, lasting connection
with listeners, who may swiftly move on to the next
podcast in search of fresh content.

Specialty podcasts can be likened to exclusive insider
bars. Patrons with very specific music preferences

visit these establishments to listen to a particular band performing on a given day. While the audience size may be smaller, the level of dedication and identification is notably heightened. This dynamic mirrors the essence of specialty podcasts. Once listeners uncover a unique "gem," their loyalty tends to persist far longer compared to what is typically observed with mainstream podcasts. Consequently, when managing a specialty podcast—commonly seen in the realm of corporate podcasts—it's advisable not to place excessive emphasis on the charts.

Charts of Apple Podcasts and Spotify

However, there are charts within podcast platforms that cater to niche podcasts, which can be quite intriguing. Let's delve deeper into this in the upcoming section.

Take **Apple Podcasts**, for instance, with its "New and Noteworthy" category. This section showcases podcasts that have been on Apple Podcasts for a maximum of eight weeks. Hence, it's crucial to publish high-quality content and promote it effectively within this initial timeframe. (We will revisit the marketing aspect in the "Podcast Launch" section.) Securing a spot in the "New and Noteworthy" category is not as challenging as it seems. With a well-crafted new podcast, strategic marketing, and a consistent release schedule, one can easily find their way into this coveted section.

Spotify features both automatic and manually curated general charts and categories. While some are algorithmically generated, others are handpicked by an editorial team who sift through numerous podcasts to create a personalized list of recommendations. Securing a spot on this list is more a stroke of luck with minimal influence on your part. The list predominantly showcases mainstream formats, often highlighting a plethora of Spotify exclusive content.

Overall, it's a fair statement to make that maintaining consistency and quality leads to a favorable ranking. Focus on consistently delivering high-quality content, as this will likely result in your podcast being well-received by the algorithms.

Factors Influencing the Ranking

What other factors influence podcast rankings? Primarily, the **number of views** on your podcast channel and the latest episodes are crucial. To excel in the charts, it's essential for your podcast to be listened to frequently. That's why we delve into specific strategies for distributing and promoting your podcast within your network in the "Advertising Channels" section.

Additionally, the **number of subscribers** to your channel plays a significant role. It's beneficial to prompt listeners to subscribe multiple times during your podcast episodes.

Platforms like Spotify and Apple Podcasts incorporate **star ratings**. Similar to Amazon, users can rate podcasts with up to five stars and provide brief reviews. Accumulating more star ratings, especially with accompanying feedback, enhances your podcast's ranking.

Another vital factor is the **listen-through rate** of your episodes. If your content is only listened to for a short duration, platforms may interpret it as less engaging, thereby affecting your ranking. Encouraging listeners to engage with your podcast for an extended period is key to improving this metric.

Paid Content and Exclusives

In addition to the regular podcasts produced by everyday users, there are some special formats worth mentioning briefly for the sake of completeness (although they are not pertinent to business podcasts).

One format includes paid content, where users can access additional material for a fee. However, this model hasn't gained widespread traction, as many individuals are hesitant to invest significant sums in podcast content.

Exclusive deals involve partnerships with specific platforms, often granted to celebrities who regularly produce podcasts exclusively for a platform. Spotify, in particular, is heavily involved in this practice. Nevertheless, this model isn't particularly appealing to standard podcasters or businesses.

Additionally, there are what are known as "originals."

These podcasts are developed in partnership with a particular platform. For instance, Spotify might engage a dedicated studio, a producer and host, or a group of influencers to create and release a podcast exclusively on its platform. Typically, these podcasts are mainstream in nature and often have an editorial focus. However, this model is generally less appealing to independent podcasters or business-focused podcasts that feature advertising content.

Paid Content   Exclusives   Originals

For independent podcasters or business-focused podcasts, establishing a strong presence is essential. Fortunately, there are numerous effective strategies to achieve this goal, which we will explore in detail in the section dedicated to advertising channels.

The Podcast Launch

Having covered how to publish your podcast on popular platforms and the crucial factors for maximizing visibility in the preceding sections, you are now ready to progress to the next stage: the podcast launch. This initial phase marks the commencement of your podcast journey, specifically focusing on the first few weeks following the release of your inaugural episode. This period is instrumental in determining the visibility of your podcast, underscoring the importance of thorough preparation.

Before the Launch

The process begins even before the official launch: Prior to releasing your initial podcast episode, it's essential to generate substantial interest within your potential target audience. Utilizing social media is the most effective approach for this purpose. To foster a high level of engagement, involve your target demographic as closely as possible in the podcast's preparation.

The key to this engagement lies in **lively interaction**. Encourage your audience to offer their input and help shape the future of the podcast. You could achieve this by prompting them in a post or story to suggest specific topics that would interest them in such a podcast. This interactive approach not only fosters a sense of involvement among your followers but also significantly increases the likelihood of them tuning in to the podcast once it's live.

During your preparations, consider sharing exclusive **behind-the-scenes content** to provide your target audience with a glimpse into the process. This may include videos showcasing the setup of your studio or early recording sessions, sparking curiosity and anticipation among your followers leading up to the launch.

For a more polished approach to the launch, you could establish a **waiting list** and compile a list of followers interested in your podcast. Upon releasing the first episode, you can reach out to them collectively, sharing the podcast link and thereby garnering a high number of initial views.

The primary aim of all pre-launch endeavors should be to maximize the viewership of your initial episodes. These episodes receive heightened scrutiny from algorithms, making them pivotal for your ranking on podcast platforms.

The First Publications

Following the preparations, you can kick off your initial publications right away. It's crucial to make a strong initial impression: Strive to craft your first episodes to be as engaging as possible.

The key is to pique your listeners' curiosity and present a novel perspective, offering them something unexpectedly captivating. You might share intriguing "mini-secrets" about your work or personal journey, or feature a standout guest.

When it comes to creativity, the sky's the limit - the primary goal is to garner clicks and encourage the maximum possible listen-through rate!

Following the debut of your initial episodes, the platforms' algorithms assess your podcast, assigning a preliminary "base score" that is then fine-tuned with each successive episode. A favorable score increases the likelihood of your podcast being featured in categories like "New and Noteworthy."

Keeping the Momentum

After your initial episodes have been released and hopefully well received, it's crucial to maintain momentum. Capitalize on the interest generated by the early episodes to engage your audience and cultivate a community of dedicated listeners.

Consistent publication is key, especially within the first eight weeks when your podcast is eligible for the "New and Noteworthy" category. Make sure to inform your audience about your posting schedule so they can anticipate it. A weekly or bi-weekly release frequency is often recommended.

However, prioritize quality over quantity. The goal isn't to churn out as many episodes as possible, as this could result in brief listens and cancellations, signaling lower podcast quality to algorithms.

Moreover, focus on steadily expanding your audience

to attract new potential listeners. Utilizing platforms such as social media can be instrumental in achieving this goal, as detailed in the "Advertising Channels" section.

Continuity   Quality   Traffic

Given the complexity of the publishing process and the ease of losing track or overlooking crucial details, a comprehensive launch checklist is provided in the accompanying materials of this book to ensure a successful podcast launch.

Advertising Channels

After you've successfully uploaded your initial podcast episode to all platforms, the most labor-intensive part is behind you. Now, the focus shifts to maximizing your podcast's reach and ensuring it reaches as wide an audience as possible. In this section, I'll outline the most efficient methods to grow your listenership and raise awareness about your podcast. We will begin by assessing your current standing and then delve into strategies involving social media platforms, paid advertising, and other promotional techniques. Additionally, we will explore collaborating with influencers, making guest appearances, and cultivating your community.

Determining Existing Reach

Before diving into planning your strategies, I suggest conducting a thorough assessment of your current reach. Begin by considering: Which channels are you currently leveraging to connect with individuals from your target demographic? Chances are, you already possess established connections within a social network, an email subscriber list, or other channels that can serve as a foundation for your outreach efforts.

To begin, let's focus on social media. Which social platforms are you currently engaging with? Both business profiles and personal accounts are valuable assets. Platforms like Facebook, Instagram, LinkedIn, and YouTube are especially effective for promoting a new podcast.

Traditional media outlets can also be a valuable avenue for promoting your podcast or specific episodes. If you have previously connected with journalists who have covered your company or work, they may be open to sharing news about your exciting new podcast project.

One of the simplest methods is **utilizing your existing channels**. Start by examining your website or, if applicable, your newsletter. How large is your audience there? Explore the best ways to tactfully showcase your podcast in these spaces—a good initial step to take.

Moreover, your **personal network** holds significant value. Are there potential influencers within your circles who could help amplify your podcast among their followers? The term "multiplier" may sound complex initially, but it essentially pertains to individuals with broad networks whose reach you can tap into through collaboration.

Social Media

Utilizing social media platforms is likely the most potent method for promoting your podcast and connecting with a broader audience. The advantage lies in your ability to construct these platforms entirely by your efforts and manage their expansion independently. However, establishing a sizable fanbase demands patience or an already substantial following that can be leveraged to expand your target demographic. A recent survey conducted by Statista documented the social media channels pertinent to podcasters and their respective market shares.

Predictably, **Facebook** leads the pack with 63% market share. Despite declining active content consumption, the platform retains a vast user base, many of whom now primarily engage through Facebook Messenger for chats. While Facebook has evolved into a multifaceted array of tools, leveraging your existing presence there remains beneficial.

Following closely at 49%, **Instagram** secures the second position as the social network with the next highest usage. Instagram is notably more specialized compared to Facebook, emphasizing emotional topics and aesthetics over "hard" subjects like politics and business. Personal everyday life content thrives on Instagram, making it ideal for consumer-oriented themes. The platform boasts robust interaction features, allowing seamless feedback collection through its stories feature related to your podcast episodes.

TikTok presently holds a 31% share, emerging as the "rising star" in social networking. The platform's rapid growth facilitates content virality, although user attention spans are notably brief. TikTok predominantly caters to individuals under 25, making it an advantageous platform if your podcast targets this demographic. Behind-the-scenes insights and concise video snippets are especially effective on this platform.

In contrast, **Twitter**, capturing 29% share, serves as a hub for a distinct variety of content. Recognized for discussions and debates on "hard" topics, the platform excels in fostering depth and ironic commentary. Users on Twitter exhibit heightened engagement with the content posted, typically representing a well-educated demographic in the middle age range. Sharing a podcast episode here significantly increases the likelihood of it being heard.

LinkedIn holds a 24% share and serves as a business-oriented network with a highly defined target audience focusing on professional themes. If your podcast caters to business clientele, LinkedIn offers a precise platform to effectively target and engage this audience. The network fosters a robust discussion culture, and its networking framework facilitates valuable feedback exchanges among users.

Formats for Social Media Promotion

How can you attract attention to your podcast on social media platforms? A popular method involves creating an audiogram, where a static image of your podcast cover is enhanced with an animated waveform to visually complement the audio. Tools like Headliner simplify this process—simply upload your episode, choose a segment, add a background image, and generate the animation. Headliner automatically generates a downloadable video file featuring the animated graphic, allowing you to showcase a compelling podcast highlight to your audience.

Additionally, you can highlight a specific quote from your episode in a text-based format using a quote tile. This format includes a photo, such as of the guest, alongside a clear and concise textual quote. Quote tiles are particularly effective on visually-focused platforms like Instagram.

When it comes to websites, you can use an embed player, utilizing an HTML code provided by your hosting platform or Spotify. By embedding this player in a suitable location on your site, visitors can directly listen to the associated podcast episode without the need to switch to another app. Importantly, views via the embed player are typically tracked within your hosting platform's statistics.

Audiogram

Quote Tile

Embedded Player

Using Paid Ads

Paid advertisements are a key consideration in the realm of social media promotion. Given the escalating competition for user attention on social platforms, especially with the rise in advertising from prominent companies, it's becoming increasingly challenging to reach interested audiences with organic content alone. To make your content stand out, you must either curate exceptional material or consider boosting specific posts through self-promotion. Most social media apps now offer direct options for post promotions. You can test the waters without launching an extensive campaign by allocating a modest budget, say €10-20, to advertise a particularly engaging podcast episode. This strategy allows you to access previously untapped target demographics within an affordable range. Even though paid ads may not consistently yield desired results, they are worth experimenting with.

Website

An essential component of your marketing strategy should be a well-rounded website. Nowadays, nearly every company maintains its own website, which tends to see frequent visitor traffic—whether people are seeking more information about your company or making purchases. Seize this opportunity to showcase your latest podcast episode by integrating an embed player as discussed previously.

Strategic placements on your website include featuring your newest episode prominently, perhaps in a small informational box labeled "Already heard? Our latest podcast episode," on the homepage. Additionally, consider linking relevant podcast episodes within blog posts that align with the article's content.

To enhance visibility, I recommend incorporating icons for platforms like Spotify and Apple Podcasts in the footer of your website alongside links to your social media channels. Placing these icons alongside links to your legal disclaimers and privacy policy increases the likelihood of visitors clicking through out of curiosity, thereby boosting visibility for your podcast channel.

For websites with a "News" section, consider enhancing it with multimedia elements like embed players featuring your current podcast episodes to offer a dynamic experience for visitors.

Newsletter

Newsletters have emerged as a vital marketing tool in today's landscape, growing in significance due to the escalating challenge of capturing your target audience's attention through social media platforms. Unlike the elusive algorithms of social media, newsletters offer a direct means of engaging with a broad audience, a digital bulletin that consistently lands in your potential listeners' email inboxes.

As a podcaster striving to connect with your target demographic through social media, you often grapple with the platforms' algorithms. These algorithms determine the visibility of your content; if your post is deemed less relevant than another user's content by the algorithm, it is likely to reach fewer individuals and struggle to gain virality. Notably, professional influencers pose tough competition in vying for potential listeners' attention.

In contrast, newsletters provide independence from algorithmic constraints, allowing you to directly reach your target audience—provided they have willingly subscribed to receive your updates.

Multipliers

A highly effective marketing strategy involves leveraging multipliers—individuals who already possess a significant reach. Your podcast guests likely have their own networks, which you can tap into for promoting your podcast. I suggest discussing episode promotion with your guest beforehand, exploring whether they can identify individuals within their network interested in the episode's topic and encouraging them to share it.

Collaborating with your guest on a brief teaser video and sharing it across both of your networks on the podcast release day can significantly amplify your outreach. By combining your audiences, you widen your potential listener base beyond what you could achieve alone. This shared approach benefits both you and your guest, as they also gain exposure through your network, potentially accessing new customers or connections. Moreover, your guest's network may include individuals who would find your podcast engaging, thereby expanding your reach further.

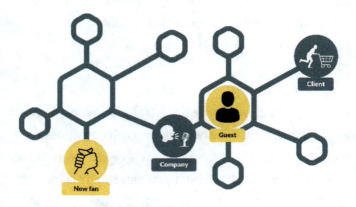

Through the reciprocal support exchanged with our guests, our network expands consistently with each new episode, culminating in our evolution into multipliers. Ideally, this progression may lead to a scenario where individuals proactively approach us to feature as guests on our podcast.

Being a Guest Yourself

Expanding your reach further involves making guest appearances on other podcasts. In addition to hosting your own guests, consider seeking opportunities to be a guest on diverse podcasts by actively reaching out to other podcasters. Ideal podcast hosts for collaboration are individuals from complementary industries, tackling related subjects without direct competition. Just as with your own podcast guests, guest appearances on other podcasts offer a seamless way to reach new audiences and enrich your community.

Community Building

We have now arrived at the final section of this chapter: community building. Having explored methods to enhance both your podcast's reach and your own outreach through various channels, it's time to delve into the distinct marketing discipline of community building. This pivotal strategy yields long-term effects and holds particular significance within the podcasting realm. In this segment, I elucidate the mechanics of effective community building.

Appreciate your Audience

A crucial aspect of cultivating an engaged community is to hold your audience in high regard. The podcasting community thrives on idealistic principles, a sentiment that becomes evident when participating in major podcast conferences. These gatherings offer a platform for podcasters to connect, share insights, and explore emerging trends within the field.

Attending such conferences has consistently highlighted the cohesive nature of the podcasting realm and the shared values among podcasters. For new podcasters seeking to establish connections within the community, it's imperative to comprehend and align with this value system to actively participate in enriching exchanges.

The podcasting community is highly interconnected, fostering opportunities for cross-collaboration. By delivering quality content through your podcast, it becomes relatively seamless to either appear as a guest on another podcast or host podcast hosts on your show. This symbiotic relationship thrives on a shared ethos of mutual support.

With its vibrancy and dynamism, the podcasting

sphere is brimming with experimentation and innovation. Many podcasters exhibit a penchant for exploring novel avenues, reflecting an innovative mindset. Thus, should you find yourself contemplating embracing a fresh trend, my recommendation would always lean towards giving it a try for the growth and enhancement of your podcast.

The podcasting community is notably inclusive and accessible, welcoming anyone to embark on their podcasting journey and intertwine with this diverse realm. Despite efforts by large corporations to govern podcast content, the notion of gatekeeping struggles to take root within this expansive and varied landscape. The multitude of voices and content genres present in podcasts attests to the openness of the community, wherein individual creators retain autonomy over their publication choices. This environment fosters a receptive attitude towards novel formats and innovative approaches.

Embodying democratic principles, podcasts serve as platforms for collective dialogues and the amplification of a multitude of perspectives, enabling individuals to express their viewpoints and have their voices heard. Unconventional or less mainstream topics find resonance within the podcasting sphere, granting them significance and space for exploration beyond traditional media conventions.

By embracing these fundamental principles, you can navigate the podcasting community adeptly, transcending mere podcast broadcasting to engage with the scene holistically. Understanding these values will not only facilitate your integration within the community but also ensure that you are embraced within this network, fostering a supportive environment where fellow podcasters provide a helping hand and backing.

Getting the Listeners Involved

Engaging your listeners plays a pivotal role in cultivating a thriving community. It's essential for them to sense a deep connection with your podcast, beyond being passive consumers, but rather as active contributors to the content. This sense of involvement fosters a stronger bond with your project, encouraging listeners to tune in to episodes in their entirety, offer comments, and eagerly share your content.

To facilitate listener engagement in your podcast venture, there are several effective strategies that I would like to outline.

Correspondence

Recations

Voice Messages

One of the simplest ways to foster listener loyalty is through emails. I recommend creating a dedicated email address for your podcast and actively encouraging your audience to share feedback, provide episode opinions, and suggest topics. This approach not only yields valuable insights from your target demographic but also invites listeners to actively contribute to the evolution of your podcast.

It's beneficial to consistently monitor reactions to your podcast. Notably, if you feature a prominent guest or cover an exclusive topic, reactions in the social media sphere can surface swiftly. You can leverage these responses as discussion points in subsequent episodes, adding depth to your content.

Encouraging listeners to send voice memos is another effective method for active participation. Given the auditory nature of podcasts, voice memos serve as a fitting format for engagement. Utilize platforms like Spotify or traditional means like WhatsApp for sending voice memos. With permission from the sender, you can incorporate these voice memos directly into your podcast, infusing your episodes with a lively, interactive element that channels your audience's unique voices.

CHECKLIST:
NEXT STEPS

As we wrap up this book, I hope it serves as a launching pad for your imaginative podcasting odyssey. The supplementary materials included alongside this book offer practical tutorials, worksheets, and templates geared towards aiding you in the hands-on application of your knowledge.

To ensure you stay organized and on course amidst the abundance of information, presented below is a concise checklist outlining the sequential steps towards the realization of your completed podcast.

Begin by crafting your target audience avatar, pinpointing precisely who your audience comprises and devising the most effective strategies to engage with them. With this foundation in place, proceed to select the podcast theme that aligns with your avatar. Contemplate an apt title and determine the format best suited for your content — be it a solo endeavor, a co-hosted venture, or an interview-based show.

Following this, initiate contact with potential guests and secure interview dates. It's advisable to commence this process early, given the busy schedules of many individuals. Planning ahead allows for adequate lead time to schedule appointments seamlessly and ensure smooth coordination.

Simultaneously, consider procuring the necessary recording equipment. In the technology section, you will discover tailored setups for various podcast formats, along with a detailed shopping list featuring specific equipment and links to recommended suppliers.

Following this, focus on crafting the audio branding for your podcast. Develop or commission an introduction and conclusion to instill a distinctive and polished identity to your podcast. Within the materials accompanying this book, access a link to our website dedicated to podcast intros, offering demos for your perusal.

With your groundwork laid, venture into producing your inaugural episode. Post-recording, you can choose to edit it independently using the free Audacity software or enlist a service such as kurt creative for production assistance. The decision hinges on whether you prefer to invest your own time or opt for external production, allocating a modest budget for efficiency.

Upon completion of the first episode, export it and upload the content, including the podcast cover, title, descriptive texts, and show notes, to your hosting platform. Once the podcast is accessible across all pertinent platforms, initiate promotional efforts through social media, your personal network, influencers, and other promotional avenues.

- ✓ **Define target group avatar**
- ✓ **Define topic, title, format**
- ✓ **Address guests and make appointments**
- ✓ **Order, set up and test technology**
- ✓ **Produce intro / outro (or have it produced)**
- ✓ **Record the first episode and have it edited**
- ✓ **Set up hosting and upload content**
- ✓ **Promote the podcast via advertising channels**

I wish you all the best in your podcast creation journey! It brings me great joy to be able to assist you through this book. For additional guidance, tips, and ample inspiration, do check out our YouTube channel and visit our website at www.kurtcreative.de. There, you can explore informative videos, insightful content, and details about our podcast production services.

ABOUT THE AUTHOR

Kurt Woischytzky studied communications management in Berlin (Germany) and then worked as a producer for the radio stations BB Radio and Radio Teddy. During the onset of the podcast boom, he initially dabbled in producing a diverse array of podcast formats as a freelancer. Subsequently, in 2019 he established his company kurt creative through which he has assisted over 200 clients spanning various industries in effectively launching their podcasts. Transitioning to a fully digital setup in 2023, kurt creative now operates globally from the vibrant hub of Madrid, Spain, serving clients worldwide.

www.ingramcontent.com/pod-product-compliance
Lightning Source LLC
LaVergne TN
LVHW051733050326
832903LV00023B/915